Managing Workplace Conflict

by Jean Lebedun, Ph.D.

American Media Publishing
4900 University Avenue
West Des Moines, IA 50266-6769 U.S.A.
800/262-2557
www.ammedia.com

Managing Workplace Conflict

Jean Lebedun, Ph.D.
Copyright © 1998 by American Media Inc.

This publication is designed to provide accurate and authoritative information in regard to the subject matter covered. It is sold with the understanding that neither the author nor the publisher is engaged in rendering legal, accounting, or other professional service. If legal advice or other expert assistance is required, the services of a competent professional should be sought.

Credits:

American Media Publishing:	Art Bauer
	Todd McDonald
Editor in Chief:	Karen Massetti Miller
Designer:	Jim Hoover
Cover Design:	Maura Rombalski

Published by American Media Inc.
4900 University Avenue
West Des Moines, IA 50266-6769

Library of Congress Catalog Card Number 98-072097
Lebedun, Jean
Managing Workplace Conflict

ISBN 1-884926-93-2

Printed in the United States of America
01 00 99   9 8 7 6 5 4 3 2

Introduction

Conflict in the workplace happens every day—and with our hectic, ever-changing work environment, it's no wonder. Because conflict is so common, each of us needs to develop the skills necessary to manage conflict productively. The good news is that when properly managed, conflict provides a chance for us to learn from each other, to improve our work methods, and to build team solidarity. *Managing Workplace Conflict* will help you handle conflict confidently so you get positive results.

About the Author

Jean Lebedun, Ph.D., is a communication specialist from Kansas City, Missouri, who deals with high-stress situations: conflict, criticism, and anger. Her clients include government agencies and major corporations. She has presented keynotes and workshops in 10 countries. Earlier in her career, Dr. Lebedun was a university instructor and a manager in a medical center.

Self-Assessment

You're about to learn the valuable career skills of how to manage conflict productively. Take the self-assessment below to determine how well you presently handle conflict.

1.	I see conflict as an opportunity.	Never	Sometimes	Always
2.	I address conflict openly, without avoiding or ignoring it.	Never	Sometimes	Always
3.	I speak directly to the key person in a conflict (rather than complaining to a third party).	Never	Sometimes	Always
4.	I listen patiently to the other side in a conflict (I don't interrupt).	Never	Sometimes	Always
5.	I separate the issue of the conflict from the feelings.	Never	Sometimes	Always
6.	I express my views without making personal attacks on the other person.	Never	Sometimes	Always
7.	I use emotional self-control during a conflict.	Never	Sometimes	Always
8.	I remain nondefensive even when someone attacks me.	Never	Sometimes	Always
9.	I am flexible in negotiating, when it's appropriate.	Never	Sometimes	Always
10.	I hold firmly to my position, when that's appropriate.	Never	Sometimes	Always

Now score your responses:
Never = 1 point each; Sometimes = 2 points each; Always = 3 points each.

Write down your total score: _____
27–30 points: Congratulations! You manage conflict effectively. Read this book for reinforcement and to maximize your benefits from conflict.

18–26 points: You have room for improvement. Read this book to build the skills you need.

17 points or less: You have major challenges in learning to manage and benefit from conflict. Read this book carefully—don't skip a single page!

Table of Contents

Chapter *One*

Taking a Positive Approach to Conflict

Chapter Objectives

▶ Identify three myths regarding conflict.

▶ Explain the benefits of conflict.

▶ Recognize the styles of conflict to avoid.

▶ Follow three techniques for focusing on the positive aspects of conflict.

Case Study

"**Learning, growing, and cooperating are goals for resolving conflict.**"
–Thomas Crum

Angela was so upset she could hardly eat her lunch. "I've had it," she complained to her friend and coworker John. "I just can't take any more of this blaring country music in the office!"

"Is this about your new officemate, Betty?" John asked.

"Right. She's driving me crazy." Angela responded. "All day long, that music is twanging away from the radio. It's been about three weeks now. I can't concentrate on paperwork, and I can't hear people on the phone. It's getting to the point where I dread coming to work!"

"Have you talked this over with Betty?" John asked.

"Well—no." Angela answered hesitantly. "I wouldn't want to hurt her feelings. She seems like a sweet person. Besides, how can I say anything now? This situation has become the status quo. I'm stuck."

How We Usually Deal with Conflict

Angela's situation isn't that unusual. Conflict in the workplace happens every day. In fact, it's not only common but also normal. Everyone has preferences, habits, and opinions. Sometimes we get in each other's way. Angela, for example, prefers a quiet work setting. Betty wants to have a simulating environment, lively with loud music.

Unfortunately, Angela is handling her conflict situation the same way many of us do—by ignoring it. Instead of discussing the issue with Betty, Angela pretends everything is okay, then complains to a third party. Betty may not know what the problem is, but she notices that Angela gives her dirty looks.

1

Ignoring the Situation

Ignoring a conflict is one of the most common responses people have when confronted with a conflict situation. Instead of actively trying to manage the conflict, we avoid the issue and desperately hope things will get better. Face it: unless we take definitive action, the situation will probably get worse.

> Ignoring a conflict is one of the most common responses people have when confronted with a conflict situation.

Conflict seldom resolves on its own. The best way to deal with conflict is through open and honest communication. The major challenge in managing conflict is to acknowledge it and take action. We need to take direct action, using assertive communication, instead of spinning our wheels unproductively.

Take a Moment

Briefly describe a conflict you have observed at work in which one or more of the people involved did not address the issue directly.

_____

_____

Now check off the negative effects that resulted.

_____ Hidden resentment

_____ Revenge

_____ Damaged team spirit

_____ Declining productivity

Becoming Aggressive

A second way that people respond to conflict is the "in your face" approach. Some people get so energized about addressing conflict that they become aggressive. See if the following scenario sounds familiar.

Case Study

■ Eric, the night supervisor, yelled at Carlos, the evening supervisor, "You'd better control those morons you have working for you!"

"What?" gasped Carlos.

"Don't play games with me," snarled Eric. "Those incompetent idiots left another mess for my night crew. We can't do our work and yours too."

Carlos answered in a low, angry voice. "Your crew doesn't do any work at night. They sit around and read magazines. Everybody in the plant knows that."

Eric deals with conflict by attacking. It's open communication, all right—but it's brutal. An attack usually leads to a counter-attack. The people involved are creating an organization that will destroy itself from within.

Take a Moment

Briefly describe a conflict you have observed at work in which one or more of the people involved did not address the issue directly.

_____

_____

Now check off the negative effects that resulted.

_____ Bitter arguments

_____ Accusations that become progressively worse

_____ Lowered job satisfaction

_____ Declining productivity

Dealing Effectively with Conflict

We've just seen two approaches to conflict that clearly don't work:

1. Avoiding or ignoring the conflict

2. Attacking and accusing the other party involved in the conflict

There is, however, an alternative. The healthy approach to managing conflict is open, yet respectful. The goal is to promote a mutual exchange of ideas. When you are able to handle conflict in this manner, you will have career skills that will serve you well in today's workplace.

> **The healthy approach to managing conflict is open, yet respectful.**

We're currently seeing a great deal of conflict on the job. Where does all this conflict come from? You'll find typical reasons listed below. Check off the ones that apply to your employment setting:

❑ Change in the workplace (arguments arise in a clash of the old vs. the new)

❑ High-stress workplace (pressure to produce, to do more with less)

❑ Unclear lines of responsibility (disagreements over who should be doing what)

❑ Lack of communication (we didn't get the message in time)

❑ Diversity in the workplace (multiplicity of viewpoints)

All of these causes for conflict reflect a vibrant, dynamic workplace. In our struggle to keep up and to keep each other informed, differences of opinions are bound to emerge. So a reasonable attitude toward conflict is simply, "It's normal." Let's go even further: *Conflict is an opportunity.*

> **Conflict is an opportunity.**

When we view conflict as an opportunity, we can see it as a signal that a problem needs to be solved. Conflict means that we need to clarify an issue, expectations, or responsibilities that have simply not been commonly understood.

Admittedly, this positive view of conflict is not prevalent in the workplace. Most people fear and reject conflict. That's because of three myths regarding conflict that have been accepted (mistakenly) as the truth.

Take a Moment

Check the myths you have accepted in the past. Can you identify where you learned these myths?

❑ It's not "nice" to have conflict.

Where you learned it:

_____

❑ Conflict is the same as a fight (it has a win/lose result).

Where you learned it:

_____

❑ A true team experiences only harmony, never conflict.

Where you learned it:

_____

The Three Myths of Conflict

Myth 1: It's Not "Nice" to Have Conflict

> When you have a valuable idea, even an unpopular one, it's important to speak up.

Many of us grew up with the advice to get along with the people with whom we work. That was good advice, but it's easy to carry it too far.

Have you developed a habitual smiling face and the dogged attitude of "I can put up with anything"? That's not fair to you—and it's not fair to the people around you. When you have a valuable idea, even an unpopular one, it's important to speak up. What does it mean to be "nice," anyway? If the only way to be nice is to go along grudgingly and suffer inside, we need another definition. Why not say that "nice" is treating others in a considerate manner? The fact is, you can be respectful of others' ideas and needs while still presenting your own side of an issue with vigor and credibility.

1

Here's the best approach to conflict: Be gentle on people and tough on issues. In this book, you'll learn exactly how to do that.

Be gentle on people and tough on issues.

Myth 2: Conflict Is the Same as a Fight (It Has a Win/Lose Result)

Do we have to have winners and losers whenever we have a conflict? Let's hope not. But you might think so if you stop to consider all of the other types of contests in which one side clearly comes out on top while the poor losers suffer defeat.

In an election, you know there will be winners and losers. In a sports event, you know there will be winners and losers. Headlines play up this effect with verbs like "trounced," "destroyed," or "ruined." One team, we learn, has "wiped out" the opposition. This fight really seems to be a war.

But the place where you work is not a political campaign or a football field. At work, the win/lose mentality is deadly. The winners gloat, and the losers grumble. Here's an example of what can happen.

At work, the win/lose mentality is deadly.

Case Study

■ Arnold and Bernetta serve on the Budget Committee. As the committee plans for the next fiscal year, one allocation in particular comes under contention. "My department needs this amount in order to accomplish our goals," Arnold explains, and he presents his data convincingly. Then he cites the inefficiency of several other departments, including Bernetta's. He insists they would not use the funds responsibly.

Bernetta gets defensive. "My department can't even survive without that allocation," she protests. But she sees that the committee members are leaning in Arnold's direction. She finally withdraws into a stubborn silence and doesn't even bother to raise her hand when the committee votes.

During the rest of the meeting, Bernetta stares at Arnold, thinking, "Okay, Mr. Hotshot. You won this time. Just wait till you call my department for administrative support. Just see who has the upper hand then."

Take a Moment

Have you seen examples of win/lose conflicts? Jot them down.

1. Situation: _____

   Winner: _____   Loser: _____

2. Situation: _____

   Winner: _____   Loser: _____

3. Situation: _____

   Winner: _____   Loser: _____

Look at a win/lose conflict like the previous example closely, and you'll see that it isn't win/lose at all. It's lose/lose. The "loser" can't wait to make the "winner" a "loser." That's why it's negative to approach conflict as a fight.

> You can manage conflicts so that both sides come out winners.

As we'll see in this book, you can manage conflicts so that both sides come out winners. The choice is yours. You can stop thinking of the other person as an opponent or enemy and make that person a partner. If both of you view yourselves as being on the same side, your conflict can end win/win.

Myth 3: A True Team Has Only Harmony, Never Conflict

Imagine that your team has a new leader. This person begins by saying, "My first rule for the team is no conflict. I will not allow any conflict." Can you recognize what just happened?

The new team leader has put a lid on the effectiveness of the group. In fact, this is now just a group and not a true team at all.

Contrary to the myth, effective teams experience conflict. They indulge in spirited arguments. They challenge each other. They question decisions. But they do so in a way that expresses respect for individual members, loyalty to the team itself, and commitment to productivity.

Contrary to the myth, effective teams experience conflict.

1

Teams know what to do with conflict. They tackle the hard work of communicating about controversial issues. Teams learn from conflict.

Finding the Positive Side of Conflict

Conflict has a positive side. Here are the benefits that will result when we manage conflict skillfully. As you read the list, check off the ones you would like to see become a reality in your workplace.

❑ We can bring up opposing ideas and know others will listen.

❑ We can have spirited arguments without attacking each other.

❑ We can resolve problems in a way that preserves the team spirit.

❑ We can find creative solutions by combining various viewpoints.

❑ We respect each other for our differences, although we don't always agree.

❑ We enjoy our jobs more—and the people with whom we work.

If these benefits have meaning for you, you now know why it's important to learn the steps for resolving conflict. It's not always easy or even pleasant. Tension usually surrounds conflict. In fact, some people let this tension get so strong that they release the energy in negative ways, as we'll see in the following section.

Take a Moment

In order to apply what you'll learn in this book, you'll need to have real-life situations in mind. Start right now by identifying one or two conflicts you are currently experiencing or have experienced recently. Write a brief description.

1. This is a conflict about_____.

   The other party in the conflict is _____.

   Here's what I have done so far: _____

   _____

2. This is a conflict about _____.

   The other party in the conflict is _____.

   Here's what I have done so far: _____

   _____

Avoiding Negative Styles of Conflict

Many people deal in negative ways with the tension that often results from conflict.

Many people deal in negative ways with the tension that often results from conflict. They develop negative styles of conflict that affect everyone, not just those directly involved in the conflict situation.

Following is a list of some of the most common negative conflict styles. As you read the list, check off the styles you have observed in your work setting. Then consider the negative impact these styles have on the entire organization. These styles of conflict are hard on everyone, not just those who are directly involved in the conflict.

❑   Firecracker
    In the midst of a conversation or meeting, someone blows up in sudden anger. Later, the person apologizes profusely. But you know it will happen again.

1

❑ **Cold shoulder**
Two people take pride in not communicating with each other. They're having a contest to see who can last longer without talking about the conflict.

❑ **Backstabbing**
Someone is congenial to you when face to face. Later, talking to others, this person criticizes you viciously.

❑ **Memory lane**
As two people discuss a conflict, one brings up a painful, unresolved issue from the past. In the heat of emotions, they forget the current problem.

❑ **Social zinger**
Someone throws verbal darts at you when other people are around. You can't figure out what the real point is because this person claims, "I was just teasing."

❑ **Trivia fights**
Two people battle over tiny decisions. They never get to the real issue, which is difficult to bring up.

❑ **Having the last word**
At the end of a conflict resolution, one person has to get in one last stinging remark before walking away. You realize that the conflict isn't really over.

Did you check some or all of the styles above? The list seems to cover a lot of ground—from exploding to refusing to talk, and everything in between. Actually, these styles of conflict have a common core: *denial.*

In a conflict situation, denial occurs when you use your energy in some way other than talking with the key person about the key issue. The result is that things get worse. The atmosphere is filled with suspicion and fear.

Denial occurs when you use your energy in some way other than talking with the key person about the key issue.

Sharpening Your Focus

For many people, conflict is a negative experience. That's why you'll have special skills when you know how to use conflict as an opportunity to learn and grow. As you read this book, you'll learn to keep your focus positive in three ways.

1. **Focus on issues, not personalities.**
   "Don't take it personally" is great advice because an objective attitude helps people stay clear-headed. They can listen better and solve problems more effectively. So talk to people about issues, using words like "deadlines," "job responsibilities," or "specifications." Avoid loaded personal adjectives like "rude," "sneaky," or "undependable."

2. **Focus on the future, not the past.**
   The true purpose of resolving conflict is to gain improved methods for the future. Emphasize the future and you'll find that people will work with you, not against you, to resolve conflict. That's because the future is always full of hope. We haven't lived it yet—so anything is possible!

Focus on solutions, not blame.

---

3. **Focus on solutions, not blame.**
   Nothing is as destructive as blame. When you make someone wrong, that person will respond with something like this: "You're worse than I am." It takes communication finesse to keep a conversation targeted at what we need to do now, not whose fault it is. Help people be the best they can be, and they will probably do the same for you.

Chapter Summary

Conflict is about differences. People have different preferences, habits, and opinions, and sometimes those differences create conflict. Because of the expanding diversity of the workforce, we're seeing more workplace conflict than ever before.

Change also creates conflict in the workplace. During times of change, we experience high stress, unclear lines of responsibility, and lack of communication. All of these realities set up an ideal environment for conflict.

Conflict can be a positive or a negative experience—it's your level of skill that makes the difference. The negative results occur if you take either of these common approaches:

1. Avoiding or ignoring the conflict

2. Attacking or accusing the other party involved in the conflict

The problem with avoiding conflict is that the conflict usually doesn't go away; in fact, it often gets worse. Attacking, on the other hand, may just seem like open, direct communication. But it's a style that makes enemies and destroys teamwork.

Many people are reluctant to deal direction with conflict because they accept these three myths about conflict as true:

◆ **Myth 1: It's not "nice" to have conflict**

Actually, all of us, including nice people, have conflict. We just need to know how to manage it properly.

◆ **Myth 2: Conflict is the same as a fight (win/lose result)**

Actually, a win/win result is possible if you use the right skills.

◆ **Myth 3: A true team has only harmony, never conflict**

Actually, teams learn and grow through using conflict positively.

Is there a positive side to conflict? Definitely! When people who work together are not afraid to say what they think, the atmosphere is dynamic and creative. People have more commitment to their jobs because they know their ideas will be listened to and considered.

Conflict can be an opportunity, but only if we know what to do—and what not to do. Here are some styles of conflict to avoid:

◆ Firecracker

◆ Cold shoulder

◆ Backstabbing

◆ Memory lane

◆ Social zinger

◆ Trivia fights

◆ Having the last word

So what is the proper way to approach conflict? Try emphasizing these three areas:

1. Focus on issues, not personalities. Let's aim for problem solving, not personal put-downs.

2. Focus on the future, not the past. Looking ahead, not back, keeps the tone positive.

3. Focus on solutions, not blame. Blame only drives people apart, but finding solutions brings people together.

Now that we've seen some of the bad and good potential in conflict, we're ready for the specifics of how to analyze conflict and how to communicate during conflict. The rest of the chapters in this book will help you build the skills you need.

Conflict is an opportunity for good things to happen—but it's not a guarantee. You must make conflict work for you.

Self-Check: Chapter One Review

Answers to the following exercises appear on page 100.

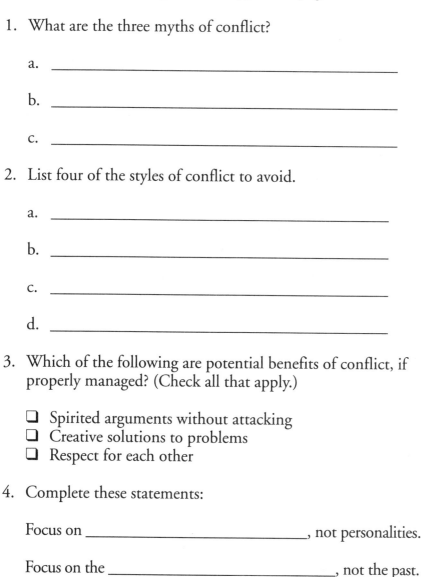

1

1. What are the three myths of conflict?

    a. _____

    b. _____

    c. _____

2. List four of the styles of conflict to avoid.

    a. _____

    b. _____

    c. _____

    d. _____

3. Which of the following are potential benefits of conflict, if properly managed? (Check all that apply.)

    ❑ Spirited arguments without attacking
    ❑ Creative solutions to problems
    ❑ Respect for each other

4. Complete these statements:

    Focus on _____, not personalities.

    Focus on the _____, not the past.

    Focus on _____, not blame.

Chapter *Two*

Analyzing Conflict Situations

Chapter Objectives

▶ Define *conflict*.

▶ Identify the two dimensions of conflict.

▶ Identify the four types of conflict.

"The chronic disease of society is equating conflict and violence."
–Kenneth Boulding

Why should you analyze conflict? Because whenever we understand something, we're more willing to deal with it. One reason so many people avoid dealing with conflict situations is fear of the unknown.

Analyzing conflict will give you a handle on it. You will be able to dissect a conflict situation and explain it. When you can see the situation objectively, you'll be able to manage your emotions and not get carried away. To help you do this, we'll consider a definition of conflict and two ways to analyze it.

Defining Conflict

Case Study

■ Oscar hands the vacation request form to Nancy, the department secretary. He is surprised to see an angry expression on her face.

"No, no," she says. "It just won't work this way. You know I have to get this form one month before you intend to start your vacation. You're giving me just 21 days notice. Sorry. Rules are rules."

Oscar protests that he needs the time off to see his mother, who is ill. He gets very agitated and starts shouting.

Oscar and Nancy's situation fits the definition of conflict to a "T." Like every good definition, this one provides not only a sound concept, but ideas for action as well. The definition is:

Conflict is a struggle between two parties who perceive their goals as incompatible.

The first part of the definition reminds us that conflict always has two sides. They may be two individuals or two groups of people. At work we often see conflicts involving two shifts, two departments, two regional divisions, or just two factions that have drawn a battle line around a particular issue.

Conflict is a struggle between two parties who perceive their goals as incompatible.

2

Take a Moment

Conflict can involve two individuals or two groups. Have you ever observed a conflict between two groups—shifts or departments, for example—in your work setting? Jot down some examples:

1. Conflict between _____ and _____

    over this issue:
    _____.

2. Conflict between _____ and _____

    over this issue:
    _____.

3. Conflict between _____ and _____

We can easily fall into the trap of regarding the two sides as two enemies. Enemies engage in war, so the result of this thinking will not be win/win. It's just plain negative to describe the conflict as "Oscar vs. Nancy."

Instead of having a clash of people, let's have a clash of ideas. Let's stay objective. Now the second part of the definition comes in handy: Conflict is a struggle between two parties who *perceive* their goals as incompatible.

Let's state the conflict like this:

■ Nancy's goal: To get a one-month notice on vacation requests

■ Oscar's goal: To give a 21-day notice on his vacation request

These are the "incompatible goals." But notice that the definition says they are *perceived* as incompatible. Nancy and Oscar see their goals as irreconcilable. It is possible to see the conflict in another way. It is possible to figure out a way for both goals to be achieved at once. Here's how Nancy and Oscar were able to use that strategy.

Case Study

■ As Nancy and Oscar talked over the issue of the vacation request, they realized several important points. Oscar realized that time was required to process paperwork through the personnel department. Nancy realized that Oscar's mother was so ill that he might be visiting her for the last time.

Nancy also realized that Oscar assumed "one month" meant submitting the vacation request in the month prior to the one in which he wanted the vacation. By "one month," Nancy had really meant 30 days from the planned vacation. But she decided to be flexible.

"I'll tell you what," she said. "I'll rush these papers through this time so you can go on your trip. This is bending the rules, but I'll send out a memo, explaining that notice of 30 days is required. That's what I'll need in the future."

The previous example was a win/win resolution because both sides achieved their goals, in a way. Nancy managed to uphold her rule and will even benefit from reinforcing the rule in writing. Oscar got his vacation, but he understands that the special treatment is for one time only.

Flexibility is the key to successful conflict resolution.

Flexibility is the key to successful conflict resolution, and it is achieved through communication and cooperation. Another ingredient is important: careful, discriminating thought. In some situations, you'll find it easy to bend. In other cases, you'll draw a line in the sand so you can live with your conscience.

As you analyze conflict, you'll often ask yourself, "Should I concede a point? Should I compromise?" We'll explore how to answer those questions in our analysis of conflict.

2

Take a Moment

Think of conflicts you have experienced. Were you willing to be flexible or not? Give examples.

1. Conflict example:

   _____

   Could you be flexible? ❑ Yes ❑ No   Why or why not?

   _____

2. Conflict example:

   _____

   Could you be flexible? ❑ Yes ❑ No   Why or why not?

   _____

According to the definition, conflict involves two parties who "perceive their goals as incompatible." In managing conflict, your job is to find ways that those goals can become compatible so that both sides can achieve part, most, or all of what they want. It's a challenge, and it definitely requires a partnership, not a war. Carefully analyzing the conflict situation will help you begin to build that partnership. Analyzing the emotions behind the conflict and allowing those emotions to be expressed are important first steps in conflict management.

Analyzing the Emotional Side of Conflict

A common complaint heard in conflict situations goes something like this:

■ "I thought the conflict was over. After we talked about what we could do, I really felt relieved. But I noticed things weren't getting any better. The conflict kept going on and on. Then we really started fighting."

Most conflicts typically have two dimensions:

1. The issue

2. The emotions

When you think a conflict is concluded, but it isn't, the problem might be that you didn't address both dimensions of the conflict. To get closure and have a sincere agreement from both sides, be sure to deal with both the issue and the emotions.

The *issue* is the source of the conflict, and we always have a triggering event that tells when an issue needs to be discussed. You've seen these triggering events frequently on the job. Someone says in a staff meeting: "I didn't get the memo about the family picnic until the day before the event. That's not enough time to plan." The issue—the timing of company communications.

The issue can usually be expressed in about five words or fewer. It's brief, like a title or headline, and states the substance of the conflict. It answers the question "What is the conflict about?"

If the issue is the "what" of a conflict, *emotions* are the "how." Ask yourself, "How do the two sides feel about this issue?" The feelings are the emotional repercussions that follow the triggering event.

You can count on seeing emotions in every conflict—sometimes strong, sometimes mild. Once you're tuned in to this dimension, you can take several steps to deal with emotions effectively:

1. Identify your own emotions.

You can count on seeing emotions in every conflict— sometimes strong, sometimes mild.

2. Listen for the emotions of the other person.

3. Allow appropriate time for emotions to be expressed.

4. Separate emotions from the issue.

Take a Moment

During conflict, do you ever have any of these emotions?

❑ Frustration
❑ Anger
❑ Confusion
❑ Disappointment
❑ Hurt
❑ Worry
❑ Others: _____

_____

Though we must deal with the emotional dimension whenever we address conflict, mixing emotions with the issue can create confusion. We can avoid this mistake by asking ourselves two questions, as illustrated in the following example.

■ Your coworker, Alice, has strong feelings for a new marketing plan she has just developed. She speaks energetically, raving on about how well it will work. You could easily get swept up in her enthusiasm. But you listen with a discriminating ear. You recognize her feelings, and at the same time you notice logical discrepancies in her plan—it's full of holes. You now have the ability to respond on two dimensions: acknowledging Alice's feelings and discussing the issue.

At this point, you are faced with Question 1: Which should you deal with first, the emotions or the issue?

You might be tempted to say "the issue" because that's the substance of the conflict. Think again, and realize that people can't deal with an issue rationally when emotions are swirling. Emotions have a way of intruding with a mental "Beep . . . Beep . . ." effect that blocks out much of the issue.

Deal with emotions first.

Deal with emotions first. You'll find that both sides can concentrate on the issue more fully after emotions have been resolved.

Now you are faced with Question 2: Who can resolve the emotions? The answer is *the owner of the emotions*. You cannot talk other people out of their emotions. But we hear these futile attempts all the time:

- "Calm down."

- "Don't be upset."

- "You have nothing to worry about."

It's better to listen with empathy, letting the other person express emotions. Be willing to express how you feel as well. Resolving emotions really means getting to vent our emotions. Expressing emotions in this way will not result in a reversal of feelings, but you can expect a sense of emotional balance.

To see how an emotional analysis of a conflict works, let's consider our previous example of the conflict between Nancy and Oscar.

Anatomy of a Conflict

Case Study

Parties involved: Nancy and Oscar

Their goals:
  Nancy—to get a one-month notice on vacation requests
  Oscar—to give a 21-day notice on his vacation request

Issue: Vacation request procedure

Emotions:
  Nancy—stubborn, upset
  Oscar—worry, fear

Both Oscar and Nancy need to give each other the chance to vent these emotions before they can resolve the issue behind their conflict.

Take a Moment

Now it's time to analyze a conflict from your life. Pick any conflict you can think of, possibly one that you observed from the sidelines. (Check the examples you wrote down on page 14 to refresh your memory.)

Anatomy of a Conflict

Parties involved: _____ and _____

Their goals:

_____'s goal: _____

_____'s goal: _____

Issue: _____

Emotions:

_____'s emotions: _____

_____'s emotions: _____

2

Analyzing the emotional dimension of a conflict can help us recognize our own feelings and give the other side an opportunity to express theirs. This is an important first step in conflict management. A second type of analysis—identifying the type of conflict—will help you respond to the issue itself.

Identifying the Four Types of Conflict

There are four basic types of conflict:

◆ Type 1: Conflict over facts or data

◆ Type 2: Conflict over process or methods

◆ Type 3: Conflict over purpose

◆ Type 4: Conflict over values

You can count on just about every conflict falling into one of these categories. Sometimes, a conflict may combine elements of two, three, or even four categories.

Identifying which type of conflict you are dealing with is valuable because:

◆ You will understand whether a conflict is simple or complex.

◆ You will direct your communication directly to the type(s) you have identified.

◆ You will uncover underlying causes of the conflict.

◆ You will know whether to be flexible or stand firm.

So, let's begin by considering each type of conflict in further detail.

Type 1: Conflict Over Facts or Data

Sometimes we have conflict because each party has different data, or a different interpretation of the same data.

Sometimes we have conflict because each party has different data, or a different interpretation of the same data. This is the kind of misunderstanding that's not supposed to happen. But even when people are trying to be clear, the message sent may not be the same as the message received, as in the Oscar and Nancy example:

■ Nancy thought her coworkers would understand that when she said "one month," she meant 30 days. Oscar assumed she meant the month prior to the one in which the vacation was to start.

Watch for expressions that are open to misunderstanding. Be sure to get a mutual agreement on what these words mean:

◆ *Majority*—Is it 51 percent, or is it more?

◆ *First thing in the morning*—What time is that?

◆ *Next year*—Is that the calendar or the fiscal year?

◆ *Shared decision making*—Who, exactly, will be involved?

Some Type 1 problems occur when people have two different sources of information.

■ LaDena is using the regulations from state law; Bob is reading federal law.

- George follows the standard procedure for performance appraisals; Edward has the newly revised procedure.

- Carl has the maintenance manual for Model 3200; Donna assumes he'll use the manual for Model 2301.

In a way, Type 1 conflicts seem simple because we can clear things up by bringing the facts to light. But we often forget to examine this aspect of conflict. We just take it for granted that everyone is reading from the same page, and interpreting it the same way.

Tip: Check for mutual understanding of the facts in every conflict, just in case it is a Type 1 situation.

2

Take a Moment

Have you seen any Type 1 conflicts lately? See if you can give examples of one or two cases in which people thought they were drawing on the same data, or thought they had the same interpretation.

_____

_____

_____

Type 2: Conflict Over Process or Methods

This type is the most common in the workplace. We have a clash on how to reach our destination. Nancy and Oscar both wanted the vacation policy to work, but she preferred the strict method and Oscar asked to bend the rules. Consider this second example:

- Michael and Andy, both frontline supervisors, agreed on the need for cost containment. Michael insisted that the best method was to use supplies more sparingly. "It's the painless way to save money," he said. Andy countered, "No, we should reduce the number of employees. That's the only way to save really substantial amounts."

This kind of conflict provides a golden opportunity. As both sides explain their reasons, they learn from each other. It's possible that the best method will emerge from a hard-hitting, point-by-point comparison. Another possibility is combining methods for a new plan.

Tip: When you know there's a conflict over methods, take the time to compare the methods side by side. Be willing to combine elements of both methods.

Take a Moment

Have you seen examples of Type 2 conflicts at work? List examples in which two sides preferred different methods to get the same result.

_____

_____

_____

Type 3: Conflict Over Purpose

This type is very serious because the two parties don't even agree on why they are doing their work. They need to clarify the purpose, or they will keep arguing every step of the way, as in this example:

■ Dee and Loma, both nurses, were putting together an in-service training program. They had conflict over every aspect of the planning—the length of the program, the curriculum, the speakers. Finally, Dee threw up her hands and said, "Let's make some decisions here. After all, we just need to get Continuing Education Units for the nursing staff."

"That's not my purpose!" said Lorna. "I want to see a measurable reduction in medication errors."

Again, conflict is an opportunity. The two nurses need to decide which purpose they can both live with. Maybe they can incorporate both purposes into their planning.

Conflict over purpose is one of those things that isn't supposed to happen. We keep asking ourselves, "Why didn't we clear this up in the first place?" The fact is, work goes so fast these days that we often jump into a project without laying out the basics (like "why are we doing this?").

Tip: When you're in the middle of a bitter conflict, check out the possibility of Type 3 conflict. Have each person answer the question, "Why are we doing this?"

2

Type 4: Conflict Over Values

This conflict is the most serious one because values are principles of life. These are the ideals that guide us, such as

◆ Honesty

◆ Kindness

◆ Preserving life

◆ Strengthening families

When you look at a list like this, you might wonder how anyone could have a conflict over values. Who could be against these things?

Controversy comes in the application of values. You may hear people using the same terms but applying them differently. One person says that in the interest of "family values," we must allow a troubled child to stay in the home of his mother and father. The opposition insists that this child will truly experience "family values" in a loving foster home.

Conflicts over values are the most emotional and the most difficult to resolve with a win/win conclusion. These are situations in which you're probably not willing to be flexible. But recognize that the other side holds convictions just as deep as yours are. Type 4 conflicts test our ability to respect other people, even when our viewpoints are different.

Conflicts over values are the most emotional and the most difficult to resolve with a win/win conclusion.

Tip: In a values conflict, be willing to stand your ground.

Types of Conflict: Your Turn to Analyze

Read the conflicts below. Analyze each by checking off the level(s) you believe are involved. Answers are on page 100.

1. "You're wasting your time," snaps Ernie. "Go out in the shop and start getting ready for the monthly inspection." Donald glares back at Ernie, because he has been told that the inspection has been delayed for a week. Ernie, however, has a memo stating the inspection is today.

   ❑ Type 1: Conflict over facts or data
   ❑ Type 2: Conflict over process or methods
   ❑ Type 3: Conflict over purpose
   ❑ Type 4: Conflict over values

2. A customer wants Jacque to coordinate a landscaping project. Jacque enjoyed working with this customer in the past when she installed plants in the lobby of her building. But Jacque has little experience in landscaping, so she asks if the customer would work with Everett, the landscape designer. The customer says no.

   ❑ Type 1: Conflict over facts or data
   ❑ Type 2: Conflict over process or methods
   ❑ Type 3: Conflict over purpose
   ❑ Type 4: Conflict over values

3. Betsy spends much of her workday convincing her coworkers to contribute to her favorite charity. It's a cause that you believe in, too, but you object to her using company time for her efforts. When you bring up the issue, Betsy yells at you: "But this is about ending world hunger!"

   ❑ Type 1: Conflict over facts or data
   ❑ Type 2: Conflict over process or methods
   ❑ Type 3: Conflict over purpose
   ❑ Type 4: Conflict over values

2

Take a Moment

Now analyze a conflict from your life. Use the same conflict that you considered on page 27, "Anatomy of a Conflict."

Briefly state the issue behind the conflict:

_____

Mark one or more:
- ❑   Type 1: Facts or Data
- ❑   Type 2: Process or Methods
- ❑   Type 3: Purpose
- ❑   Type 4: Values

Chapter Summary

Analyzing conflict is an important first step in managing conflict situations. When you can analyze something, you feel more objective and in control. Controlling emotions is especially important in managing conflict.

We began our analysis with this definition of conflict: *Conflict is a struggle between two parties who perceive their goals as incompatible.*

Note that they *perceive* the goals to be incompatible. The fact is, both parties can usually "win" if they communicate and cooperate. Most of all, they need to be as flexible as possible.

When we analyze conflict, we need to consider two dimensions: the issue and the emotions. The proper way to balance the two dimensions is to deal with emotions first, then move to the issue. The reason for letting feelings go first is to clear the air. Listen to the other person's frustration. Express your own frustration. People often need to vent, especially after conflicts have been allowed to fester.

When you believe that emotions have been expressed, you can start working to resolve the issue. Many people tackle this part too early. If emotions are still raging, nobody can be rational and logical.

A second useful analysis is to identify the type of conflict. There are four basic types of conflict. Just about every conflict situation fits one or more of these types:

◆ **Type 1: Conflict over facts or data**
The two sides in the conflict have two sets of facts, or two different interpretations of these facts. This level represents a basic misunderstanding, yet it is one we often overlook. But now you can be smart and double-check whether there is agreement on such things as statistics and definition of key terms.

◆ **Type 2: Conflict over process or methods**
Most conflicts at work are about how to do our work. Both sides have the same goal in mind, yet they prefer different ways of getting there. If people really listen to each other, they may find merit in both methods. They will probably find a way to blend ideas together creatively.

◆ **Type 3: Conflict over purpose**
This is a difficult conflict, requiring open, honest discussion. Both sides will learn that they don't even agree on why they are doing a particular project. They may be able to compromise or choose one purpose over the other. Both sides must agree on a mutual purpose so they can make definite plans about what they are going to do.

◆ **Type 4: Conflict over values**
A conflict over principles of life is the most emotional of all conflicts. While you can show respect for people who hold values different from your own, you are probably not willing to change your values on the spot. You can be flexible in some conflicts, but not in this one.

When you take the time to determine these types, you will be able to keep your communication focused on what's relevant. You will get to the heart of what the conflict is really about.

Analyzing conflict is a big step forward. As long as you're analyzing, you're staying calm, rational, and emotionally balanced. In the next chapter, we'll build on this process of analyzing. You'll see the specific steps you can take as you prepare for a conflict resolution with a specific person.

Self-Check: Chapter Two Review

Answers to the following exercises appear on page 101.

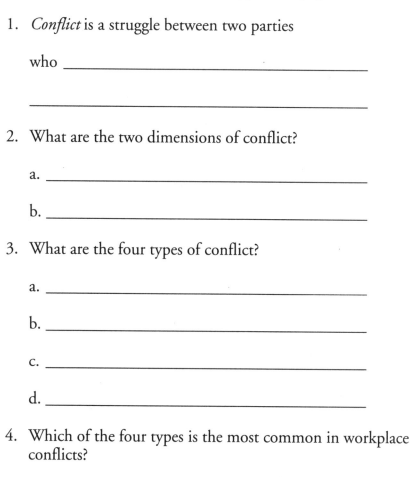

1. *Conflict* is a struggle between two parties

    who _____

    _____

2. What are the two dimensions of conflict?

    a. _____

    b. _____

3. What are the four types of conflict?

    a. _____

    b. _____

    c. _____

    d. _____

4. Which of the four types is the most common in workplace
    conflicts?

    _____

Chapter *Three*

Setting the Stage for Productive Conflict

Chapter Objectives

▶   Use the 3 Rs of conflict.

▶   Take long-range steps for managing conflict.

▶   Prepare to manage a specific conflict.

> "Courage is the price that life exacts for granting peace."
> –Amelia Earhart

Long before conflict ever occurs, you need to get ready for it. Does that sound like a negative attitude? Actually, it's a realistic attitude. Conflict is not a matter of "if," but a matter of "when." Conflict *will* occur between you and the people you work with. By getting ready, you're programming your next conflict to be a productive one.

Using the Three Rs of Conflict Management

You can prepare for conflict by using the Three Rs, the principles for sound conflict management:

◆   Responsibility

◆   Relationship

◆   Real Problem

Taking Responsibility

Picture a typical situation at work. Person A has a problem with something Person B has done. Does A tell B about it?

Often, instead of telling B, A tells C. That's talking *about* the person rather than to the person. But it feels pretty good. So A decides to tell D, then E, then F—and the story gets bigger and more negative with each retelling.

You can see what's happening. Person A is getting sympathy instead of a resolution to the conflict.

Taking responsibility means communicating directly instead of backstabbing. But people get quite creative at finding reasons for not being direct:

■ "I couldn't say anything. I don't want to hurt her feelings."

■ "I can't bring this up to my boss, for heaven's sake."

■ "I'm afraid he'll get mad if I say something."

■ "Why waste my breath? She won't listen to me anyway."

■ "She'd just take this the wrong way."

■ "He would get back at me later."

■ "I've waited too long. I can't bring it up now."

These excuses are all statements of irresponsibility. Responsibility, on the other hand, compels you to take constructive action.

The first step in taking responsibility is to take the initiative in addressing the conflict. Bring it up in a nonthreatening way by citing the issue. For example,

■ "I'd like to talk with you about our differences regarding the budget proposal."

The next step is to communicate responsibly during the conversation with your conflict partner.

3

Compare the two columns below to see the difference between communicating responsibly and irresponsibly. How would you

Irresponsible	Responsible
Lois can call me if she wants to talk about it. She knows my number.	I'm going to call Lois to see if we can work this out.
Claude, what you're saying just doesn't make sense.	Claude, I'm not following this very well. Let me ask you a few questions.
Tim, you let me down again.	Tim, what happened?
You messed this up again, didn't you?	Perhaps I didn't make myself clear. Here's what I meant to say…
You're not listening!	Let me put this another way . . .
Describe the effect:	**Describe the effect:**
_____	_____
_____	_____

describe the effect of each of these styles of communication? You may have described the "Irresponsible" column as being negative, blaming, attacking, insulting. Doesn't sound like a team player, does it?

You may have described the "Responsible" column in terms like ownership, cooperative, respectful, creative. This approach definitely reflects a team spirit.

When you speak responsibly, you set the tone for the other party.

Being responsible means that you are part of the solution, not part of the problem. And there's a hidden benefit. When you speak responsibly, you set the tone for the other party. You certainly can't make others communicate in a responsible way, but it is more likely if you lead the way.

Take a Moment

Test your ability to identify responsible communication. In each pair below, check the statement that is responsible. Answers are on page 101.

1. _____ I'd like to hear your side of the story.
   _____ Quiet down and listen to me.

2. _____ You don't know what you're talking about.
   _____ Help me understand where you got your information.

3. _____ As far as I'm concerned, this is the only way to look at it.
   _____ Can you help me find any holes in my logic?

3

Maintaining Strong Relationships

Case Study

■ Enzo is the kind of man people both admire and fear. He's very experienced in his chosen field of accounting, he stays up to date with the newest technology, and he always has an informed opinion. Unfortunately, when Enzo expresses his opinions, he always has to be right. He can never admit that he might be wrong, and he insists on being right at the expense of others.

Enzo has been known to hammer his point brutally, humiliating the person he's talking to. His eyes narrow into slits, and his voice turns to ice when he says things like: "The latest information, which of course you didn't bother to read . . ."

Have you ever worked with someone like Enzo—someone who prefers winning a conflict to preserving a relationship? Enzo's tactics may build his ego, but destroying relationships can destroy your ability to manage conflict.

What's so important about relationships? Relationships help us get the job done. When people want you to succeed, they give you cooperation every day and special consideration in a crisis. When people are against you, they sabotage your efforts in subtle—but powerful—ways.

If you want to use the positive approach to conflict, take care of relationships in two ways:

1. Build relationships *before* conflict happens.

2. Preserve relationships *during* a conflict.

You can build relationships before a conflict by taking a personal interest in your coworkers. Everybody likes to be treated as an individual and to be appreciated for unique contributions.

During a conflict, be careful how you state your case. It is possible to be right and yet not make the other person wrong. You can state a correction tactfully and preserve the relationship. Enzo might say something like this:

■   "You're wrong. You're just flat wrong—again."

The more tactful version would sound like this:

■   "I have information different from yours. Look at page 5 in the latest report from the central office. It says 32 percent."

In a Type 1 conflict (facts or data), you can state accurate information without demeaning the other person. Use a similar approach in a Type 4 conflict (values). State your view, but avoid personal judgements, such as "you're immoral," "you're unethical," or "you're dangerous."

Showing respect for the other person will maintain the relationship, no matter how severe the clash of ideas may be.

Take a Moment

Rewrite these statements in a way that will maintain a relationship.

1. Those figures are just plain wrong. I can't imagine where you ever dug them up.

   _____

2. You can try to fix the equipment that way, but don't come crying to me when it falls apart.

   _____

3. Permissive attitudes like yours are what's wrong with this country today.

   _____

Focusing on the Real Problem

Strange as it seems, people in conflict often shift their attention to secondary conflicts that have nothing to do with the real problem. You've probably witnessed those "trivia fights" (one of the styles of conflict to avoid, covered in Chapter Two) in which one person snaps at another over a small point. It's a way to release energy when the real issue is difficult to talk about.

■ Denny started a petty argument with Carmelita over who should turn the lights off at the end of the day. What he really was worried about was the travel expense reports. He feared that Carmelita was padding the amounts she claimed for meals, but he knew the conversation was potentially threatening.

Another way we avoid the real issue is by attacking someone personally rather than stating the issue. You may often be tempted to think: "But the problem is the person!" Don't let it be. Translate your concerns to an issue that you can state objectively. Then you're ready to speak up.

> People in conflict often shift their attention to secondary conflicts that have nothing to do with the real problem.

3

■ Denny, for example, should avoid attacking Carmelita's integrity. He should talk about the issue: allowable expenses for meals when traveling. The conversation should cover such questions as:

- How much does the company allow per day for meals?
- Does this amount include alcoholic beverages?
- Does this amount include buying a meal for a guest?

Another way we get sidetracked from the real problem is by concentrating on a symptom rather than the underlying cause. When a particular event triggers a conflict, ask yourself what the cause of that event is.

■ Sunny, the director of marketing, overheard the end of a telephone conversation her administrative assistant, Anne, was having. It was clear that Anne had been interviewed by a local television station.

"I can't believe this is happening," thought Sunny. Then she asked herself, "What is the cause?" She decided that the real problem was a lack of guidelines on how much authority Anne was supposed to have in dealing with the media. Sunny realized that this particular event was a symptom of a larger problem.

"Anne," Sunny said, "we need to talk about guidelines for working with the media."

Take a Moment

The next time you experience conflict, ask yourself the following questions:

1. Am I willing to bring up a sensitive or difficult issue?

2. Have I planned how to state this issue objectively, avoiding personal attack?

3. Have I moved from thinking about a symptom to concentrating on the cause?

Long-Range Planning for Conflict
Writing a Mission Statement

Does your organization have a mission statement? If your answer is yes, pat yourself on the back. If not, plan to take steps immediately.

A mission statement is commonly recognized as good business practice and an essential element for team building. Writing a mission statement can also be an effective long-range planning technique for managing conflict. Consider the following example:

3

■ At a staff meeting in a medical clinic, conflict was raging. Two physical therapists argued bitterly, and then a nurse tossed in some destructive comments. All of the participants were territorial and fiercely competitive. Suddenly someone said in a quiet tone, "Wait a minute. What would be in the best interests of the patient?"

Everyone was quiet and thoughtful. How could they miss the most obvious criterion for making their decision? As the discussion resumed, they all seemed more willing to cooperate.

The mission statement for the clinic was "Compassionate care for those in need."

Some mission statements may be longer, but the basic requirements are always the same:

◆ Express a higher purpose.

◆ Make it easy to remember and restate.

◆ Encompass all tasks and personnel.

◆ Focus on the people you serve.

Because the mission statement focuses on patients, customers, or clients, it unites everyone on the team. That unity really pays off during conflict. In spite of their differences, everyone involved has the mission in common. Finding a resolution becomes possible, although not always easy.

> **Because the mission statement focuses on patients, customers, or clients, it unites everyone on the team.**

To start preparing for conflict before it occurs, take these two steps to support your mission. First, reinforce the mission in your workplace. Don't let it be just pretty words in a fancy frame on the wall. Talk about it and—most of all—live it.

Second, if you do not have a mission statement, ask for a meeting in which interested representatives can put together such a statement. Get people thinking about "Why do we do what we do? What is our ultimate purpose?" When people see the big picture, they can be professional and positive in the way they manage conflict.

Take a Moment
Take a Moment Can you state the mission for your organization? If not, what can you do to see that a mission statement becomes a reality?

Short-Range Planning for Conflict

Building Your Courage

Developing a mission statement is an effective way to begin dealing with conflict in the long term. Other skills and techniques can help you in the short term when you are directly confronted by a conflict. Two of those techniques are building your courage and developing your communication skills.

Many character traits are involved in managing conflict: respect for others; responsible behavior; a sense of service, openness, and honesty. Let's add one more to the list: *courage*.

Knowing when you need to overcome your fear and take the risk is an important part of conflict management.

Why do you need courage to manage conflict? Because effectively managing conflict means taking risks. Sometimes the issue or the person involved may seem so threatening that you want to shy away from the risk. Knowing when you need to overcome your fear and take the risk is an important part of conflict management.

It's true that not every risk is worth taking. In order to be courageous, not foolhardy, you can play the "What If?" Game. This is a practical way to decide if you want to address the conflict or not.

44

Let's see how the game works. Imagine that you have a conflict with your boss. Pose these questions to yourself (here are some possible answers).

The "What If?" Game
1. What if I don't bring up the conflict?
    The worst that could happen:
        Problem escalates.
        I feel more and more frustrated.
    The best that that could happen:
        I don't have to face the boss.

2. What if I do bring up the conflict?
    The worst that could happen:
        The boss thinks I'm getting out of line.
        The boss gives me bad work assignments as punishment.
    The best that could happen:
        The boss admires my assertiveness.
        The boss appreciates learning my perspective.
        I get answers to my questions.
        We agree on how to handle things in the future.

The analysis above leads to the conclusion that you should use your courage to face your boss directly. This is usually the result of the "What If?" Game. Only a tiny percentage of conflicts are the kind where keeping your mouth shut is smart. Most conflicts are an opportunity we need to seize.

3

Take a Moment

Now play the "What If" Game using a conflict you are facing. Should you address the conflict or ignore it?

The "What If?" Game
1. What if I don't bring up the conflict?
   The worst that could happen:

   _____

   The best that could happen:

   _____

2. What if I do bring up the conflict?
   The worst that could happen:

   _____

   The best that could happen:

   _____

Developing Your Communication Skills

All conflict is resolved by communication.

Now that you have bolstered your courage, you're ready to prepare for a specific conflict. All conflict is resolved by communication. To communicate most effectively, consider the Three Ws of communication: decide *who, when,* and *where* regarding that communication.

◆ **Who?** Speak to the *key person.*
   The key person is the person who can help you solve the problem. Remember that we often complain to someone else instead of the key person in order to get sympathy. This is why you'll need to talk yourself out of the common excuses for not approaching the key person:

   • She'll just yell at me.

   • He's higher in authority than I am.

   • We haven't gotten along well in the past.

46

Use your courage. There are just two choices here: Speak directly to the key person, or forget the conflict. Address it or drop it.

◆ **When?** Discuss the issue *within 24 hours.*
A triggering event lets you know that you have a conflict. For example:

■ José finds a note from his coworker Danielle. She asks that he handle the revision of the new policy manual on his own. "That's not how we agreed to do it," he says to himself, gritting his teeth.

José needs to talk to Danielle within 24 hours. If he waits longer, his frustration may build to hostility. Or he may get into a pattern of procrastinating about important issues.

Keep in mind that the 24-hour guideline does not say "the sooner the better." Take time to collect your thoughts and decide what you really want to say. You may need a brief cooling-off period before you approach the other person. You can even sleep on the issue. Just don't put it off too long.

◆ **Where?** *A neutral place* is a good choice.
A neutral place puts both sides on an equal footing. Pick someplace that is not the "home territory" of either person. A conference room or empty office are both possibilities.

These long-term and short-term techniques can help you manage just about any conflict situation you may encounter. Your goal is to create a setting that allows each person to share ideas openly. If one person dominates, the chances of a win/win conclusion are diminished.

3

Chapter Summary

Being proactive is an important first step in conflict management. One way you can remain in charge of the conflict situation is by practicing the Three Rs of Conflict:

◆ **Responsibility**—Don't wait for the other party to come to you; take the responsibility to initiate the conflict resolution. Be sure to speak directly to the other party. We often do exactly the opposite when we talk about the other party.

◆ **Relationship**—Form close relationships with people so you have a positive context to draw on when conflict comes up. During the conflict, couch your communication in terms that will preserve the relationship. Don't make the person wrong. Don't make the person your enemy.

◆ **Real problem**—Look beyond the symptom or the surface behavior to find the basic problem that should be solved. True, it may be a sensitive issue, one that's difficult to talk about. It's all right to say, "It's not easy for me to bring this up." Only if we address the real, underlying problem can we get a real, lasting solution.

You can set the stage for resolving conflicts by taking both long-range and short-range steps. Long-range planning means establishing a mission that will unite all team members. Make the mission statement short so it's easy to remember. But it's even more important to put the mission into action. Practice it. Live it. If everyone shares the mission, they will actually be on the same side when a conflict arises.

Short-range planning is needed when you face a specific conflict. You're probably trying to build the courage to address (not avoid) the conflict. Play the "What If?" Game by asking yourself a series of questions:

◆ What if I don't bring up the conflict?
What is the worst that could happen?
What is the best that could happen?

◆ **What if I do bring up the conflict?**
What is the worst that could happen?
What is the best that could happen?

By thoughtfully answering these questions, you'll know exactly what to do. Almost always, the advantage lies in facing the conflict. Your next step is communicating.

To communicate effectively, plan carefully. These are the key issues:

◆ **Who?**—Speak to the key person. Don't be sidetracked with excuses that the person is unapproachable or that the other person should really make the first move. The responsibility falls on your shoulders. Use your courage to speak up.

◆ **When?**—If you talk with the key person within 24 hours, you'll avoid the common problem of letting a small conflict grow until it becomes unwieldy. Nip it in the bud.

◆ **Where?**—Select a place to meet with the key person. A neutral setting where neither of you has ownership helps to level the playing field.

Now you've done everything you can to set the stage, using sound principles, long-range planning, and short-range planning. In the next chapter, we'll consider a four-step model that will organize your communication with the key person.

3

Self-Check: Chapter Three Review

Answers to these questions appear on pages 101 and 102.

1. What are the three Rs for managing conflict?

    a. _____

    b. _____

    c. _____

2. A mission statement can help during conflict because

    _____

    _____

3. In preparing to address conflict, what are the three "W" questions to ask yourself?

    W_____?

    W_____?

    W_____?

4. To effectively manage a conflict, be sure to speak to the _____ person.

5. Address the conflict within _____ hours.

Notes

3

Chapter *Four*

Resolving Conflict in Four Easy Steps

Chapter Objectives

▶ Use the Four-Step Process for Conflict Resolution.

▶ Negotiate on common ground, not on positions.

▶ Make sure you get a dependable commitment.

▶ Choose among five possible outcomes.

"Conflict is a dangerous opportunity."
–Robert Bolton

Let's celebrate what you've accomplished so far in managing conflict. You now know how to:

1. Keep your focus positive by concentrating on issues, the future, and solutions.

2. Avoid the styles of conflict which are actually a denial of the conflict itself.

3. Define conflict as "perceived incompatible goals."

4. Analyze the two dimensions in a conflict.

5. Analyze which of the four levels are in a conflict.

6. Be responsible in initiating the resolution to a conflict.

7. Build the relationship with the person involved with you in the conflict.

8. Determine what is the real problem.

9. Use the "What If?" Game to build your courage.

10. Prepare for conflict by asking who, when, and where.

So you've analyzed, built your courage, and even made an appointment with the key person. Now what do you say and do?

Using the Four-Step Process

You're ready to use the Four-Step Process for Resolving Conflict. Following this process will help you organize your interaction with your conflict partner. The chapter will take you step by step through the conflict-resolution process, even suggesting words you can use.

Remember, though, that this is a model, not a script. You can adapt the words to your personal preferences. As you talk with the other party, you may spontaneously get a better idea than what you had planned in advance. Let the conflict resolution become a joint venture for both sides.

4

Let's see the Four-Step Process in action, then break it down into the individual parts that you will be using.

Turning Down the Radio: A Case Study

Angela had spent three miserable weeks with her new officemate, Betty. Although Angela liked Betty, she hated the loud country music Betty tuned in on the radio. Angela complained to her friend John, and he posed a leading question: "Have you talked this over with Betty?"

Case Study

Angela made some excuses as to why she hadn't talked to Betty. But she also thought a lot about the point John was making. She decided to face the conflict directly, so one afternoon, she said, "Betty, could we talk about the music that's playing on the radio? This is important to me."

Betty said she was in the middle of a project, but she would have time in the afternoon, right after lunch. They agreed to talk.

After lunch, Angela opened the conversation by asking Betty why she played the radio all day. To Angela's surprise, Betty explained that she considered the music to be a screen, shutting out voices and even "internal noises" in her head. The music helped her concentrate. "I'd never thought of that," Angela said.

Angela explained that she was used to a quiet office environment, especially since she had so many contacts on the phone. "The music drowns out my callers' voices, and I can't understand what they're saying." Betty was surprised to hear this.

Together, they started working on possible ways to achieve a good working atmosphere for both of them. They came up with more than a dozen ideas, including:

■ Betty could wear earphones when listening to the music.

■ Angela could wear protective headgear that shuts out sounds.

■ They could ask their employer to build a soundproof wall.

■ They could arrange their schedules so only one person would be in the office at a time.

What they finally came up with was a combination of the most feasible ideas. It turned out that Betty liked easy-listening music as well as country, and Angela liked it too. So Betty said she would try a new station. They also decided to have no music at all from 9:30 to noon, since that was the time in which Angela took most of her phone calls.

They agreed to live with the plan for a week, then meet on Friday to discuss how well it was working. They acknowledged that some changes might be needed.

Can You Find the Four Steps?

Now that you've seen the Four-Step Process in action, see if you can identify each step. You'll be looking for the following:

1. **Your Turn** (inviting the other person to speak first)

2. **My Turn** (now I get to make my case)

3. **Mutual Planning** (working together to explore solutions)

4. **Follow Through** (taking action and evaluating the success of the resolution)

Use the lines below to identify the portions of the dialog where the steps occur.

1. Your Turn: _____

   _____

2. My Turn: _____

   _____

3. Mutual Planning: _____

   _____

4. Follow Through: _____

   _____

Here are some suggested answers:

1. **Your Turn:** Angela opened the conversation by asking Betty why she played the radio all day.

2. **My Turn:** Angela explained that she was used to a quiet office environment and couldn't hear people on the phone.

3. **Mutual Planning:** The two worked together to generate ideas for creating an atmosphere in which they could both work comfortably.

4. **Follow Through:** They agreed to work with the plan for a week, then meet to discuss it on Friday.

Now let's look at the Four-Step Process in greater detail.

Following the Four-Step Process

Step 1: Your Turn

What can Angela say to start off her meeting with Betty? She begins by thanking Betty for her willingness to discuss the situation and suggests two important ground rules for their discussion:

■ Each person will listen to the other without interrupting.

■ The two of them will search together for a solution that satisfies them both.

Angela asks for Betty's agreement on the ground rules, then proceeds with Step 1: Your Turn. She can invite Betty to go first by saying something like:

■ "I'd like to hear your side of the story."

■ "Please tell me your thinking on your issue."

■ "I'd like to understand your position. Could you explain it to me?"

This is, admittedly, an unusual way to start conflict resolution. Most people start by insisting, "I'm going to tell you a thing or two!" The trouble is that imposing your view on someone sets up a win/lose tone.

On the other hand, letting the other person go first shows restraint and respect. It also has two benefits, one related to the emotional dimension and one related to the issue.

◆ **Benefit 1:** Listening to the other person helps you truly understand the issue from his or her view. We usually think we know where the person stands, but there will always be some surprises. You'll hear something that has more validity than you expected.

◆ **Benefit 2:** Listening to the other person allows a release of feelings. The other person has a chance to vent. Picture Betty explaining why she plays the radio. When she sees that Angela is sincerely listening, Betty is not defensive. She has nothing to defend; she is not being attacked. Feelings are balanced, not explosive.

Letting the other person go first truly defuses a potentially hot situation. You've set a positive tone for the entire conflict resolution. Here's what you need to do while the other person is speaking:

◆ Listen without interrupting.

◆ Show sincere interest by asking questions when appropriate.

◆ Hear the person's entire story.

◆ Paraphrase when the person has finished.

As you can see, Step 1 of the Four-Step Process draws on the skills known as *active listening*. Why is this a good beginning? The person you're dealing with now knows: "I've had a chance to lay my ideas on the table. I was not interrupted or attacked. Somebody really listened." Now you have the basis for working out a settlement. Paraphrasing what the person has said proves that you heard the other person. This statement is not an agreement; it's an acknowledgment:

> **Step 1 of the Four-Step Process draws on the skills known as *active listening*.**

> 4

■ "If I heard you correctly, you're saying that playing the radio helps you concentrate on your work."

You just want to summarize what you heard, saying the major points in neutral words.

Take a Moment

How developed are your listening skills? Here are some skills necessary for active listening. They are especially helpful during Step 1 of the Four-Step Process. Check those skills you already use.

❏ Encouraging ("Go on," "I see")
❏ Making "listening noises" ("Uhm-hum")
❏ Asking questions ("What time did that happen?")
❏ Paraphrasing ("Let me summarize what I just heard.")
❏ Changing facial expression when appropriate
❏ Leaning forward
❏ Nodding
❏ Making eye contact

Did you leave many skills unchecked? Make plans to develop them further.

Step 2: My Turn

When Betty has finished speaking, Angela introduces this second step by saying, "May I tell you my side of the story now?" It's a courteous way to begin, and it shows she values the relationship. She doesn't believe in dominating the conversation; she believes in fairness and equality.

> **It's best to have each person's side of the issue stand out distinctly.**

Angela's goal now is to present her case, not give a rebuttal of the viewpoint she just heard. It's best to have each person's side of the issue stand out distinctly. Argument or debate can come later.

Here are some guidelines for completing Step 2 successfully:

◆ Get to the point; be brief.

◆ Focus on the issue; avoid personal accusations.

◆ Speak your view firmly and persuasively.

◆ Include feelings ("I was frustrated when . . . ").

When you work through Step 2 in your own conflict situation, you will probably experience a sense of relief at getting to state your case without attacks, corrections, or nit-picking. Setting the ground rules (listen without interrupting) really pays off.

Step 3: Mutual Planning

> **The heart of conflict resolution is finding a plan both people can live with.**

The heart of conflict resolution is finding a plan both people can live with. This step has two phases: *brainstorming* and *negotiating*.

Brainstorming is a well-known process in which people generate as many ideas as possible without commenting on the worth of the ideas. This is "blue sky" thinking. Evaluation comes later.

Angela and Betty use brainstorming to generate ideas during their meeting. Together, they come up with more than a dozen possibilities on how to handle their conflict. They use the right approach: List as many ideas as you can. Go fast. Let ideas build on each other. Write down anything that's offered. Go for quantity.

Take a Moment

Have you ever participated in brainstorming? List some examples:

_____

_____

Is there anything you like about brainstorming?

_____

_____

What results have you observed?

_____

4

You will find that something subtle happens during brainstorming: The parties in conflict begin to work together. They might say, if asked, "This is *our* list of ideas." Granted, they don't have a final solution yet, and they haven't ironed out all the difficult details. But they have let brainstorming accomplish the following: they are on the same side.

Without this mutual process, what could happen? A fight, that's what. After the first two steps, each side might start insisting "My way is better!" Angela might demand, "Stop playing that radio." Betty might dig in her heels and declare, "No way!"

Brainstorming pulls both sides away from the power-play style of conflict resolution by providing a structure for interaction. They're not competing; they're cooperating.

Brainstorming also pulls both sides away from the common mistake of trying to find a "right" answer too soon. Immediately coming up with a solution is dangerous because one person will probably dominate (that's win/lose). By listing a quantity of ideas to consider, we see the possibilities that were not obvious at the start.

> **Something subtle happens during brainstorming: The parties in conflict begin to work together.**

Conflict starts, after all, as *perceived* incompatible goals: Angela wants the radio off; Betty wants the radio on. But there are some creative possibilities, and that's what mutual planning is all about.

After brainstorming, the parties can begin negotiating. This is the time for evaluating the possible solutions, raising objections, answering those objections, and combining ideas.

When you negotiate, you make a choice. You can either *negotiate on positions* or *negotiate on common ground.*

Negotiating on positions means pitting the two people's positions against each other. One side or the other will win. Either Angela will win or Betty will win. You can predict all the negative results: resentment, bitterness, the wish for revenge. But many people do not think beyond negotiating on positions. Creativity is required to even consider the other method: negotiating on common ground.

You can begin to negotiate on common ground by simply asking the question *What do we have in common?*

What a refreshing idea! Commonality now becomes the cornerstone for the resolution. Maybe what you have in common is the mission of the organization. If the mission says something like "The customer comes first," you now have something that you share. Start crafting your action plan based on that mission.

Sometimes, however, you'll find common ground that's more down-to-earth. Angela and Betty shared one practical priority: having a workable office environment. This kind of common interest can become the test for the success of the action plan: does the action plan achieve a good office environment for both people?

Take a Moment

Think about conflicts you have observed. In your experience, which method is most common—negotiating on positions or negotiating on common ground?

What is usually the result of conflicts that are negotiated on positions?

_____

_____

You may find not one but several points that you have in common with your conflict partner, as in the following example.

4

■ Bernie and Leon started out in opposition. Bernie was certain that 8 a.m. was the best time for the staff meeting, and Leon was convinced that 4:30 p.m. was the best. Then they asked, "What do we have in common?" They discovered that they both wanted:

Case Study

1. A convenient time when most people could attend.

2. A time when people could give full attention to the meeting.

3. A fast-paced, efficient meeting.

Discovering their common interests helped Bernie and Leon develop a sense of cooperation. They started evaluating each proposal by the three common interests they had identified. This emphasis kept their negotiation objective because it avoided the "do it my way" approach.

Their analysis revealed that an afternoon meeting was better because more staff members were in the office at that time, back from their morning sales calls. "Let's try the 4:30 meetings for three weeks," suggested Leon, "then talk about how well it works."

Take a Moment

Identify a conflict that you are currently experiencing at work—or one that you are observing. (One of the examples you listed on page 14 would be a good choice.) List the two sides involved:

_____

_____

Now ask the question, What do they have in common? See if you can come up one or as many as four possibilities.

_____

_____

_____

_____

Brainstorming and negotiating are two important parts of the mutual planning step. Here are two more important things to remember about this step:

1. There may be some tension at times. That's okay. Be willing to bring up opposing ideas in a respectful way. Use responsible communication, such as "I look at that in a different way than you do."

2. You may need more than one meeting. In a simple issue, like loud radio music, a conversation of 20 minutes or so may suffice. But a complicated issue will require multiple meetings, possibly involving other key players. It's your job to keep working through the various aspects of the larger issue while remembering to keep walking on common ground.

Step 4: Follow Through

A frequent complaint about conflict resolution is that it just doesn't last. It's all talk and no action. People get together, express themselves, negotiate, agree—then nothing happens.

You have two ways to ensure that something really does happen. First, get an agreement in specifics. You will, of course, adapt this idea to your situation, but it will sound something like this:

■ "Okay, so I'll do this . . . and you'll do that."

Pin down dates, times, and behaviors. Angela and Betty, for example, planned to keep the radio off between 9:30 and noon. That's better than a description like "during the later part of the morning."

People usually follow through when they know exactly what's expected. Use numbers, such as specific times, dates, or amounts, as much as possible. Then be sure to confirm this agreement with strong words delivered with direct eye contact:

4

■ "Thank you for your commitment."

■ "I'm counting on you."

Here's a second way to make things happen: schedule an evaluation meeting. Within a day or a week, you'll meet to discuss the success of the plan. This is a time to say thanks for the cooperation, or to make adjustments, or talk about additional problems that have arisen. One fact is clear: the follow-up meeting holds people accountable.

Now let's review the entire Four-Step Process. Remember that following these steps organizes your work for you, allowing both sides to be heard and plan together for the resolution to the conflict.

Four-Step Model for Conflict Resolution

1. **Your Turn**

    "I'd like to hear your side of the story."
      Listen without interrupting. Show sincere interest.
      Hear the person's entire story. Paraphrase when the
      person has finished.

2. **My Turn**

"May I tell you my side of the story now?"
    Get to the point; be brief.
    Focus on the issue, avoiding personal accusations.
    Speak your view firmly and persuasively.
    Include feelings.

3. **Mutual Planning**

"What are the possibilities?"
    Brainstorm for a quantity of ideas.
    Save evaluation for later.
    Let ideas build on each other.

"What do we have in common?"
    Identify the mission or a shared priority.
    Raise objections and deal with them.
    Prepare an action plan.

4. **Follow Through**

"Thank you for your commitment."
    Specify who does what by when.
    Schedule an evaluation meeting.

Five Possible Outcomes

When you have a resolution to a conflict, you'll find that it falls into one of these five possible outcomes:

1. Withdrawal

2. Agree to disagree

3. Acquiescence

4. Bargaining

5. Collaboration

All are win/win outcomes. But each is appropriate in some circumstances, and not in others. When you understand these five outcomes, you will be better able to negotiate a settlement that is right for a given situation.

1. **Withdrawal**
   This outcome occurs when both sides agree to drop the conflict entirely. They discuss the issue for a while, only to realize that it's not really worth the effort. What seemed important a few hours earlier now looks unimportant. Both sides agree: let's not spend any more time on this. We have more important things to do.

   When is this outcome appropriate? When the issue is low priority.

   Withdrawal occurs when both sides agree to drop the conflict entirely.

2. **Agree to disagree**
   This outcome provides closure in cases that couldn't end any other way. Two people have compared their views, only to find they are completely opposite in their thinking. They're deadlocked. But they also realize that nobody is requiring their agreement. They can just "live and let live."

   When is this outcome appropriate? When consensus is not required.

   Agreeing to disagree provides closure in cases that couldn't end any other way.

4

3. **Acquiescence**
   This outcome occurs when one side accepts the proposal of the other side. It's not giving in, because it's a genuine choice. No force or coercion is involved.

   Maybe you changed your mind as you listened to the other person's ideas. You openly say, "I vote we do it your way." Or maybe you want to build goodwill. If you feel reasonably comfortable with the other person's proposal, you may go along with it in interest of the long-term working relationship.

   Acquiescence occurs when one side accepts the proposal of the other side.

   Here's another possibility: You recognize a power differential. In this case, you acknowledge to yourself that the decision is out of your hands. In a conflict with your manager, for example, you may realize that your logic is not sounding very convincing. You choose to do what your manager requires. Be gracious about it:

   ■ "Thanks for hearing me out. I do have a strong opinion, and at the same time I recognize your authority. Count on me to support your decision."

65

So acquiescence is not a weak option; it's a conscious choice. And sometimes you'll choose *not* to acquiesce, even in dealing with your manager. In a Type 4 conflict (values), you will probably draw the line if your ethics are involved.

When is this outcome appropriate? When one of three possibilities occurs:

◆ You change your mind.

◆ You want to build goodwill.

◆ You recognize a power differential.

Bargaining is a midpoint between what the two people proposed in the first place.

4. **Bargaining**
This outcome is a midpoint between what the two people proposed in the first place. They strike a bargain in which each side has traded concessions. Person A offered $30,000. Person B demanded $40,000. They settled on $35,000.

This strategy works in issues that involve money, deadlines, or physical space. There has to be something measurable to divide approximately in half.

When is this outcome appropriate? When the issue can be measured and divided. Numbers must be involved.

Collaboration occurs when the two sides in the conflict use synergy to blend their ideas into a new plan.

5. **Collaboration**
This outcome occurs when the two sides in the conflict use synergy to blend their ideas into a new plan. They put their ideas together in a way that neither person could have accomplished alone. Collaboration emerges from creativity. It is the highest-quality resolution to conflict, but the conditions are not always conducive to this outcome.

Collaboration takes time. Other outcomes—like withdrawal or acquiescence—will be quicker. But creativity must be nurtured. The people involved must have the ability to search for new answers, to listen patiently, and to stimulate the best in each other.

When is this outcome appropriate? When two conditions are present:

- Enough time is available.

- Both people have high-level communication skills.

Take a Moment

In conflicts you have experienced in the past, have you used any of these outcomes? Check the ones you have used.

❏ Withdrawal
❏ Agree to Disagree
❏ Acquiescence
❏ Bargaining

4

Chapter Summary

Managing conflict becomes so much easier when you have an outline to follow. That's the advantage of following the Four-Step Process: you can plunge in, knowing that you'll do everything in the right order.

- **Step 1: Your Turn**
  Begin by saying to the other person, "Your turn. You go first." It really disarms the other person to know that you truly want to understand without assuming or prejudging. As you use your active listening skills, you learn what the opposition's case is all about, and you give the person a chance to vent. Paraphrase to check if you listened accurately.

- **Step 2: My Turn**
  Begin this step with the statement "May I tell you my side of the story now?" As you explain your views, include both the issue and your feelings. Describe the problem without blaming. You want to make sure your conflict partner really listens to what you have to say. That's probably what will happen, especially since you set the tone by listening first.

◆ **Step 3: Mutual Planning**
Begin by putting your heads together for brainstorming. Generate as many options as possible to avoid dead-end thinking or "my way is the only way" positions. Then move to negotiating in order to make a final, mutual decision.

The key to effective negotiating is to find the common ground. Otherwise, each side keeps trying to overpower the other side to achieve a win/lose result. Instead, finding the common ground allows two people to build on a foundation in which they both believe.

What do two people in conflict have in common? Sometimes it's as big as the team mission they both made a commitment to long ago. Sometimes it's a list of practical points, such as meeting deadlines and staying within budget. Aim for three or four points that you have in common. Construct an action plan that is true to those points.

◆ **Step 4: Follow Through**
Now it's time to state a definite agreement: who will do what by when. Be as specific as possible. Lock in the agreement with an intense moment when you say, "Thank you for your commitment. I'm counting on you."

The goal is to make sure both parties follow through and act responsibly. Another way to achieve this goal is to schedule an evaluation meeting. This way, you can sit down to discuss if the agreement is working or needs to be revised. People tend to follow through when they know there will be a face-to-face meeting later.

The outcome you jointly choose will be one of the five that are listed below. All are acceptable. Just select the one that fits your situation.

1. **Withdrawal**—When the issue turns out to be a low priority, both sides decide to just drop the whole thing.

2. **Agree to disagree**—When consensus is not required, both sides decide to acknowledge their differences and still maintain respect.

3. **Acquiescence**—Maybe you changed your mind as you listened to the other person. Maybe you recognize their seniority—or maybe you just want to preserve goodwill. The point is that you (or one of you) has a good reason for saying, "I'm going to go along with your view on this."

4. **Bargaining**—When the issue can be measured and divided, you just decide to "split the difference." Each side wins half.

5. **Collaboration**—When enough time is available and the people involved have high-level communication skills, this outcome is possible. The two people, who started out in an argument, now come up with a new, creative plan of action. They sincerely call it "our plan."

When you use the four-step model to achieve one of these outcomes, you are managing conflict like a pro. In the next chapter, you'll extend your skills even further. You'll learn special skills to use in those tense, angry times in conflict when things seem to be getting out of hand.

4

Self-Check: Chapter Four Review

Answers to these questions appear on page 102.

1. What are the steps of the Four-Step Process for Conflict Resolution?

   a. _____

   b. _____

   c. _____

   d. _____

2. Brainstorming is helpful during conflict resolution because

   _____

   _____

3. You must make a choice:

   Negotiate on _____
   OR
   Negotiate on _____

4. *Collaboration* is one of the five possible outcomes of a conflict situation. Collaboration involves the following (mark all that apply):

   ❑ Synergy

   ❑ Creativity

   ❑ High-level communication skills

   ❑ Quick use of time

Notes

4

Chapter *Five*

Developing Strategies for High-Stress Times

Chapter Objectives

▶ Gain emotional self-control during conflict.

▶ Remain assertive, not aggressive, under pressure.

▶ Use any of the six special skills when necessary.

"People and
things do not
upset us.
Rather, we
upset ourselves
by believing
they can upset
us."
–Albert Ellis

So far, everything we've covered about managing conflict has been based on this premise: *Cooperate, don't compete.*

In fact, one of the five possible outcomes of conflict—collaboration—is the logical extension of cooperation. The point is to work together rather than against each other. It's your responsibility to lead the way. When you listen first, the other person will probably listen to you. When you treat someone with respect, that person will probably treat you with respect too.

Does it always work? No. Some people just won't cooperate even though you are doing everything right.

You'll need special skills for dealing with these people. They may fall into the category of "difficult people," those who are chronically (and predictably) hard to work with. Or they may be individuals who are having a very bad day. You'll know you're faced with challenges when someone does one or more of the following:

◆ Attacks

◆ Accuses

◆ Calls you names

◆ Manipulates

- Exaggerates shamelessly

- Demands

- Threatens

Take a Moment

Do you work with any people whom you consider difficult?
What do they do? List some of their frustrating behaviors
below.

_____

_____

_____

_____

5

Getting the Right Mind-Set

Imagine that you are out fishing on a lovely spring day. As you
sit on the bank of the stream, you feel a tug at the end of your
line. There's a fish down there! Now consider this question:

■ Who or what caught the fish?

Many answers are possible: the bait, the hook, the pole.
Consider another answer:

■ The fish caught itself.

Although all the other elements were present, the real cause was
the fish itself. The fish opened its big mouth and took the bait.

Do you ever "take the bait"? Do you ever "get hooked"? Most of
us would admit that this happens when difficult people use
high-pressure tactics. In these cases, we usually say things like
"He pressed my hot buttons!"

Although the difficult person may say something excessive like "You idiot!" the choice to get frustrated is yours.

Take another look. Remember that the fish hooked itself. You press your own hot buttons. You hook yourself. Although the difficult person may say something excessive like "You idiot!" the choice to get frustrated is yours.

It's true that difficult people select tempting bait to dangle in front of you (they took notes in the past when you got upset). But the choice to get emotionally hooked—or not—is yours.

This is good news. You can choose not to get hooked. You can choose to stay calm and rational. Yes, your heart may be racing, but you don't have to fall apart and become an emotional basket case.

Let's compare the old way of thinking to the new way:

Old Way of Thinking	New Way of Thinking
She made me angry.	I became angry.
He upset me.	I was upset.
They humiliated me.	I felt humiliated when I heard those comments.
He insulted me.	I took it as an insult.
She manipulated me.	I fell for her manipulation.

The goal of the new way of thinking is twofold:

◆ Taking responsibility for your reactions

◆ Gaining emotional self-control.

In a moment, we'll look at six strategies that can keep you from getting hooked.

Take a Moment

Have you ever made any statements similar to those listed under the Old Way of Thinking on the previous page? If so, write one below.

_____

Now, rewrite the sentence to reflect the New Way of Thinking.

_____

Avoiding the Hook

You can avoid the hook. The following six strategies can help you deal with difficult people without getting caught in their negative traps. Those strategies are:

1. **Sorting** (choosing words or other aspects of a communication to which you will not respond)

2. **Fogging** (stating a vague acknowledgment)

3. **Time Out** (stating an exact time to resume talking)

4. **Broken Record** (repeating your point in a calm, convincing manner)

5. **Requesting** (using an "I" statement to express what you want, need, or prefer)

6. **Flushing** (responding to what is said, not what is meant)

5

Strategy 1: Sorting

What Might Happen
During a conflict, the other person says, "You idiot! Can't you just tell me who the client is?"

What You Can Do
You can choose to mentally sort out, or ignore, the ugly word "idiot." That word is the bait. It's the other part of the comment that's relevant to the conflict. So you choose not to respond to "idiot" and you say instead, "Yes, I can tell you that the client is Acme Trucking."

> You can choose to mentally sort out, or ignore, ugly words.

Be careful of your nonverbals. Say your statement calmly, with a level, even tone of voice. Keep your facial expression neutral rather than twisted with sarcasm.

Sorting is a skill that helps you identify what is worth your attention. You avoid responding to excessive language or tone of voice. Your choose your priority in the communication.

Caution
When you're using the sorting technique, don't say you're sorting. It might be tempting to explain: "I'm not going to answer that last remark." Don't. When you explain, you show that you're hooked. You sound defensive. Just calmly and self-confidently answer only the part of the person's comment that you choose to consider important. You're in control of your own communication and your own emotions.

Take a Moment

Read the first two examples of sorting below. Then fill in the rest of the exercise. Suggested answers are on page 102.

- Someone says: "You're lying to me. You didn't put that contract in the mail."
  You say: "I put the contract in the mail on May 21."

- Someone says: "Just quit your pathetic whining and tell me when the deadline is."
  You say: "The deadline is today at 4 p.m."

1. Someone says: "You'd better ask the obnoxious Brian Anderson to return my call."

   You say: _____

2. Someone says: "Are you telling me the new software didn't arrive yet? You must be out of your mind."

   You say: _____

3. Someone says: "These figures can't be right! You're too young to know what you're talking about."

   You say: _____

Strategy 2: Fogging

What Might Happen

During a conflict, the other person says, "I demand an answer now! Do I get the 10 percent rate or not?"

What You Can Do

Sometimes people try to push you into a corner. It's hard to think straight in these situations. But when you realize that you need more time to make a decision—spread some fog.

Fog is vague and wispy. It's not a definite "yes" or "no" because you just don't have that kind of clarity yourself. Fogging uses statements like, "I'm going to bring this issue to the committee. I'll call you with that information by 3:30 tomorrow afternoon."

> When you realize that you need more time to make a decision—spread some fog.

That's not an answer, but it's a commitment to get an answer. It's the best you can do in some situations. Be sure to follow through exactly as you have promised. The purpose of fogging is to buy some time, not give the person the brush-off.

When you can give a definite answer, of course you should do so. But don't feel forced to say something in haste that you'll later regret. Use fog when you need to:

◆ Check the facts and figures.

◆ Check with a person in higher authority.

◆ Include other people in the planning.

◆ Wait for other developments.

◆ Receive a phone call with updated information.

◆ Think things over and weigh your decision.

Caution

Prepare for rejection. The person you're speaking to doesn't like fog. This is probably someone who has perfected pressure tactics and expects them to work. You'll get more pressure: a louder voice, stronger words. But if you have the strength of your convictions, you won't get hooked. After all, you're buying time to get the highest quality information you can. It's all in the other person's best interests anyway.

5

Strategy 3: Time Out

What Might Happen

During a conflict, tempers flare. The situation escalates. People lose their self-control.

What You Can Do

Whenever you think, "We're not getting anywhere. We need to get away and cool off"—you're right.

Call a break before things get out of hand. The choice of timing is yours. Trust your good judgment. Whenever you think, "We're not getting anywhere. We need to get away and cool off"—you're right.

You can call a time out in a one-on-one communication or in a meeting involving several people. Just be sure you speak firmly when you announce the break. Don't sound tentative or unsure. And don't forget to specify a time to resume so everyone knows that you're not backing down from the issue.

Your announcement might be:

■ "Let's take a break now. We'll resume in 30 minutes, right here in the conference room. I'll see you then."

Caution

Avoid adding a statement of attack. This kind of attack is common, so you could easily follow a bad example you've heard: "Let's resume in 30 minutes, *when you've learned some manners.*"

The last part of that statement hits below the belt! Edit it out. Avoid saying "when you've calmed down," "when you can behave like an adult," or anything of the kind. These attacks tend to make people defensive and put them on the counter-attack.

What you're hoping for, of course, is that the other side *will* calm down during the time out. Give this process a chance to work. If you feel doubtful, propose some ground rules when you get back together. Put these in terms that are specific and nonpersonal. For example:

■ "From here on, I suggest we follow two ground rules:
1. We'll keep our voices at a normal volume, and
2. We won't use any four-letter words.
Would you agree to that?"

Take a Moment

Think back on situations in which you have seen someone call a time out.
1. Have you seen it done the right way?
2. Have you seen it done the wrong way (with an attack)?

Strategy 4: Broken Record

What Might Happen

During a conflict, the other person refuses to acknowledge your statements or explanations, even after you have given complete details.

What You Can Do

Play a broken record. State your point calmly and repeatedly in spite of the opposition you hear. After all, at this point in the conversation, you've reached your bottom line.

If you use this skill too early, you'll sound stubborn and pig-headed. The broken record is appropriate only after you have explained, explored, and taken ample time to answer all objections. Early on, you had hoped for collaboration. Now you realize that you must stand your ground.

Your reasons for being so firm may be ethical, legal, or procedural. The point is that you have nothing more to offer. So repeat your point:

You:	I need your signature on the form.
Other person:	Oh shut up. That wouldn't do any good.
You:	I need your signature on this form, please.
Other person:	Well, I'm not going to sign and you can't make me.
You:	Please sign the form—that's all I need.

Notice that you can vary the wording so as not to sound mocking. But you're really saying the same thing. You're not arguing, just being persistent.

> State your point calmly and repeatedly in spite of the opposition you hear.

5

Persistence pays off. After about the third or fourth time you've made your point, people will probably do what you're asking—or at least consider it. Don't expect them to like it. The broken record is a way to stand firm, not a way to make friends.

Caution
When using this strategy, watch your nonverbal communication. Keep your vocal tone respectful and don't let that glaring, defiant look settle on your face. Keep your hands relaxed, not clenched into fists. These nonverbals make all the difference in remaining assertive, not aggressive.

Take a Moment

You've probably used the broken record—if not at work, then at home. Describe one or two situations:

_____

_____

Were you able to keep your voice calm?

Did your persistence pay off?

Strategy 5: Request

What Might Happen
During a conflict, the other person engages in extreme verbal or nonverbal communication, such as shouting, name-calling, or fist-shaking. You decide not to sort it out this time.

What You Can Do
Sometimes it's best to state what you need, clearly and firmly. It's honest, it's straightforward—the essence of assertiveness. Be sure to use an "I" (not a "you") statement:

■ "I want you to lower your voice."

■ "I want you to call me by my name."

■ "I want us to stay focused on this issue, nothing else."

If "you" had been the first word of the sentence, it would probably have ended aggressively:

■ "You are . . . rude and inconsiderate."

Keep it responsible with the "I" opening. And keep it positive, asking for an improvement rather than directly blaming.

Caution
Leave out any disclaimers, such as "I hope you won't be offended when I say this," or "Maybe I'm a little too sensitive about this." Disclaimers sound weak and wimpy.

Strategy 6: Flushing

What Might Happen
During a conflict, the other person makes an extremely exaggerated statement.

What You Can Do
You can flush out the truth. Encourage the person to acknowledge the exaggeration in order to steer the conversation back to practical matters.

Flushing means that you respond to the exact words the person used. Respond to what is said, not to what is meant. Take it very literally.

The exaggerated statement might be:

■ "These people are all idiots. Let's fire every one of them."

Your response could be:

■ "So you want me to fill out termination papers on all 58 employees?"

Here's what you'll probably hear in return:

■ "No, no. I guess I really went over the edge on that one. I'm just so upset."

The effect was that you brought the conversation back down to earth. Now the two of you can go on with your conversation in a sensible way.

Caution
Don't be sarcastic. You don't want this person to become angrier. Make your statement in a flat, serious tone. Your goal is to help the person hear the impact of what he or she just said.

These six strategies can help you resolve most difficult conflict situations. Using them can help you preserve relationships and keep a conflict situation from escalating into a battle.

Take a Moment

For each item below, check which of the six strategies is used in the response. Answers are on page 102.

1. "Tell me where you stand on this. Stop beating around the bush!"

   Response: "I'm going to read your proposal one more time and give it careful thought. Will you be in your office in 30 minutes if I call you then?"
   ❑ Sorting
   ❑ Fogging
   ❑ Time Out
   ❑ Broken Record
   ❑ Request
   ❑ Flushing

2. "This incident report you submitted looks like a two-year-old wrote it. Do you really expect me to believe that the electricity was off for over an hour last night?"

   Response: "Yes—it was off from 7:10 until 8:20."
   ❑ Sorting
   ❑ Fogging
   ❑ Time Out
   ❑ Broken Record
   ❑ Request
   ❑ Flushing

3. "Maybe we should just burn the whole place down and collect the insurance money."

   Response: "Do you think there would be some legal ramifications if we did that?"
   ❑ Sorting
   ❑ Fogging
   ❑ Time Out
   ❑ Broken Record
   ❑ Request
   ❑ Flushing

5

Chapter Summary

This chapter has presented you with six strategies to use when conflict becomes stressful. You're bound to have conflict from time to time with "difficult people." They may be chronically difficult or just having a bad day. Either way, they will yell, attack, or manipulate.

At these times, your job is to stay cool. You need to gain emotional control. How is this possible? First, by realizing that nobody can upset you without your permission. You can choose to stay calm because you know what to do. That's where the six strategies come in. They give you substitute behaviors so you don't fly off the handle and say words you'll later regret.

The six strategies are assertive, not aggressive. They will help you avoid insulting or demeaning the other party. You will stand up for yourself without putting anybody else down. Here are your choices:

1. **Sorting**—You choose to respond only to part of a communication and to ignore the rest. The part to which you respond is important and worthy of your attention. The part you ignore may be a nasty little dig, a negative label like "stupid," or a sarcastic tone of voice. Don't get hooked on the negative elements of communication. You know how to sort out the content of the message that needs to be answered.

2. **Fogging**—You choose to buy some time by giving a vague reply. You state that you'll make your decision later or that you'll double-check your information. Just be sure that you do get back to the person, exactly as you promised. Fogging gives you some time to collect your thoughts.

3. **Time Out**—You choose to take a break to restore calmness to a situation. Trust your instincts on this one. When you recognize that emotions are running high enough to become dangerous, call a time out. Let both sides retreat, think about what's happening, then get together again at a specified time. You're giving everybody, including yourself, an opportunity to be mature.

4. **Broken Record**—You choose to repeat your point because it's the best you have to offer. Whether you use identical words or a paraphrase, be sure your voice is calm. As you firmly restate your point, even in face of argument, you show your persistence and self-confidence. Just be sure that you have a good reason for drawing your line in the sand.

5. **Request**—You choose to ask for more acceptable behavior with an "I" statement. You do this because you've decided you can't sort out the behavior. So you can say, "I want you to lower your voice," or "I'm asking you not to use that language with me."

6. **Flushing**—You flush out the truth by responding to the literal words you hear. Sometimes people exaggerate. If you take these statements literally, you can help the other person realize what's going on. When you answer any extreme statement very seriously, you'll probably hear something like, "Oh, I guess I am getting carried away. I'm just so upset."

5

Let's face it: difficult people make conflict more challenging. While you can't control what other people do, you can control what you do. Don't let difficult people control you!

In the next chapter, we'll discuss how to live with conflict in the long run. If you can predict the pitfalls, you'll be ready for anything!

Self-Check: Chapter Five Review

Answers to the following questions appear on page 103.

1. When sorting, be sure to
   a. Explain what you're doing.
   b. Ignore part of the communication.
   c. Apologize.

2. Fogging is a
   a. Vague acknowledgement.
   b. Double message.
   c. Brush-off.

3. When calling a time out, include
   a. The time to resume.
   b. The names of difficult people.
   c. A "you" statement.

4. Why does the broken record usually work?
   a. Persistence.
   b. Sarcasm.
   c. Loud voice.

5. A request should open with
   a. "Stop that . . ."
   b. "You are . . ."
   c. "I want . . ."

6. When flushing, your goal is to "flush out" the
   a. Mission statement.
   b. Truth.
   c. Mistakes.

Notes

5

Chapter *Six*

Living with Conflict

> "We find comfort among those who agree with us—growth among those who don't."
> —Frank Clark

So far, we've seen how to use the Four-Step Process for Conflict Resolution and take appropriate steps for dealing with difficult people. In this final chapter, we'll consider how you can be ready for the unexpected. Despite your best intentions, conflict situations don't always go as planned. What if the process breaks down? In this chapter, we'll consider some of the most common pitfalls. Here's what happened to Albert, an engineer. He did everything right in managing conflict, but he still hit a snag.

Albert's Conflict: A Case Study

Case Study

Albert knew he had a serious conflict on his hands. He had spent two long weeks researching and writing a report requested by his new manager, Thelma. When Thelma passed out the report at the conclusion of the staff meeting, Albert was stunned. On the front page, he saw Thelma's name as author. His name didn't appear anyplace in the report. When the meeting ended abruptly, he asked Thelma if they could talk later about the report. They agreed on a 1:30 meeting.

Walking back to his office, Albert mentally reviewed some questions about conflict:

- Who?—He was glad he had chosen to talk to the key person rather than complain about her to others.

- When?—He had made an appointment within 24 hours of the triggering event.

- Where?—Thelma had accepted his suggestion of a neutral place, the conference room, and he felt he could speak out openly.

When they met, Albert described the Four-Step Process to Thelma:

1. Your Turn

2. My Turn

3. Mutual Planning

4. Follow Through

He told Thelma he wanted to understand why his name was left off the printed report. "I really need for you to explain this to me," he said.

Thelma started off calmly: "I've always worked in a system where the manager's name appeared as the sole author. It's the proper procedure. This is a delegated task; I'm the person in charge."

As she continued, the pitch of her voice went up, and she sounded more and more emotional. She reacted as though her authority as a manager had been questioned. Albert was glad he had given her a chance to vent. When she finished, he paraphrased what she said. Then he started expressing his opinion. Albert's experience had been just the opposite of hers.

"Here at ABC," he said, "my name has always appeared as junior author, just below the name of the manager. I deserve credit for my work."

Thelma started interrupting while Albert talked. She corrected his statements and tossed in comments like, "That's ridiculous." She sounded very upset. Albert thought, "This isn't working. She already had her turn. What can I do now?"

Albert has encountered one of the major pitfalls that can occur in a conflict situation. Luckily, as we'll see, even these difficult situations can be handled effectively.

6

Handling Conflict Pitfalls

Pitfall 1: Getting Carried Away with Emotions

Letting the other person go first will usually defuse emotional hot spots. You want your conflict partner to be able to listen attentively when you take your turn. If that doesn't work, you just start over again.

Albert needs to stop and listen to Thelma. He can ask sincere questions:

■ "What is your reason for saying that?"

■ "Could you explain that, please?"

■ "Could you help me understand?"

It's back to Your Turn again. Give it more time. Let the person explode. You may find that you're hearing the same point repeatedly. Just listen, listen, listen. You want the person to get empty so you get a "yes" when you ask: "May I tell you my viewpoint now?"

> **You want the person to get empty so you get a "yes" when you ask: "May I tell you my viewpoint now?"**

But what if you are the one who gets carried away emotionally? Wait for the My Turn step, then express yourself in an honest, nonthreatening way:

■ "Bear with me; I'm pretty upset."

■ "It's very hard for me to talk about this."

■ "I know this isn't your fault. I'm mad at the situation."

During this process, avoid blame. Avoid apologizing for having feelings. Give yourself a chance to vent, just as the other person did.

Take a Moment

Do you ever feel extremely emotional during conflict? What are the signals (dry mouth, fast heartbeat, etc.)?

_____

_____

How have you handled these emotions in the past?

_____

_____

Pitfall 2: Aiming for a Quick "Right" Answer

To each person in a conflict, the "right" answer is "my" answer. At least, that's how the conflict starts. But when people start sharing ideas, they usually discover the truth in the old saying, "There are two sides to every story."

Taking the time to go through the Four-Step Process leads to cooperation. That's what happened in Albert and Thelma's conflict—after he allowed her to vent her emotions a second time. Eventually, they discovered the two sides to the controversy:

> **Taking the time to go through the Four-Step Process leads to cooperation.**

6

Albert wanted to be listed as junior author because

1. That's what his previous manager had done.

2. He believed he deserved printed credit for his work.

Thelma wanted only her name to be listed because

1. That's what she had done in the past, at another company.

2. She planned to give Albert verbal recognition in a brief announcement at the next staff meeting.

Together, they started brainstorming, as part of the Mutual Planning step. They finally came up with a way to combine their ideas: At the next staff meeting, Thelma would verbally explain Albert's role in researching and writing the report and express full appreciation for his work. In future reports, Albert's name would be listed on a "Credits" page.

Cooperation takes more time, more work, and more communication than the "do it my way" approach. But when both people "buy in" to the resolution, the result is worth the effort.

Take a Moment

In a conflict, are you willing to take the following steps?

❏ Listen with an open mind.

❏ Find something valid in the other person's view.

❏ Combine your ideas and theirs, whenever possible.

❏ Brainstorm to generate possibilities.

❏ Seek a resolution both of you can accept.

Pitfall 3: Getting Stuck on Positions

Remember that there are two ways to work out a conflict:

◆ Negotiate on positions.

◆ Negotiate on common ground.

> When people get stuck on positions, each insists, "I won't budge an inch."

When people get stuck on positions, each insists, "I won't budge an inch." Then they have an image to maintain. It seems that making a concession would appear to be weak. They get more firmly stuck.

Here are four ways to get unstuck:

1. Be patient. Try to break the deadlock with probing questions:

    ◆ "What do we have in common?"

    ◆ "What is the mission of this organization?"

    ◆ "How can I help you meet your needs?"

2. Be willing to make a concession to start the ball rolling. Find a small point where you can be flexible—or even make a major concession and ask that the same consideration be shown to you.

3. Be open to a time out. Postpone the negotiations. Both of you may have a new perspective when you meet again. Taking a fresh look at things can really help.

4. Be open to asking a third party to step in. This is the last option, to be used only after you have tried every possible way to get a resolution on your own.

   Select someone both of you respect. Agree that you'll follow what this person says to do. Then present the dilemma and accept the decision of the mediator. While this is not truly "Mutual Planning," it does give you a way out.

Pitfall 4: Breaking Promises

The effectiveness of your efforts will be most apparent after the conflict situation has been resolved. Do you get the follow-through that was promised?

When promises are broken, you'll be glad you had a precise agreement to which you can refer. ("Okay, so I'll do this and you'll do that.")

If you believe a promise has not been kept, talk to the other person about it. Ask what happened to the agreement. Be calm and firm. Do it in private. Make it clear that you remember the commitment and you expect it to be honored. If necessary, use the broken record technique to reinforce your point. You can now consider a back-up plan in which you discuss the *consequences* of the other person's inaction. This is not a threat: the consequences are simply a matter of cause and effect, as in this example:

6

If you believe a promise has not been kept, talk to the other person about it.

■ "If this action does not happen [cause], I will speak to a higher authority [effect]."

Consequences vary, depending on the situation. Possibilities include:

♦ No longer doing business with the person.

♦ Proceeding on your own without the person's involvement.

♦ Writing up a disciplinary procedure.

In each case, you're stating what you will do if the other person does not follow through.

Make it easy for the person to cooperate with you. Make it hard for the person to let you down.

While you can't make somebody be responsible, you can create favorable conditions. Make it easy for the person to cooperate with you. Make it hard for the person to let you down.

Take a Moment

Look at the list below and check off the pitfalls you have observed in the past. Now be prepared: they may happen again.

❑ Pitfall 1—Getting Carried Away with Emotions

❑ Pitfall 2—Aiming for a Quick "Right" Answer

❑ Pitfall 3—Getting Stuck on Positions

❑ Pitfall 4—Breaking Promises

Surviving the Ups and Downs of Conflict

Conflict resolution isn't always textbook perfect. But, as you have seen, there are plenty of steps you can take to get things back on track. Be patient. Have faith in the process. Most of all, have faith in yourself as a person who is willing to do what it takes to get a win/win result. Now that you've studied all these skills involved in managing conflict, you're ready. Knowledge is power, and you certainly have the knowledge of what to do about conflict.

Will there now be less conflict in your life? Probably not. In fact, *you will probably have more conflict in your life*. How can that be? Simply because of your raised awareness. It's the same as learning a new word and suddenly seeing it all around you. You wonder how you ever got along, not knowing what that word meant. Now you'll now see—or admit to seeing—more conflict around you. But the good news is that you know what to do about it.

Angela and Betty Three Years Later

Angela and Betty have now been working together (in the same small office) for about three years. They laugh sometimes about how their working relationship started—pretty rocky.

Case Study

"I had that radio playing all the time, and I didn't even realize it bothered you," says Betty. "Thank goodness you were willing to bring it up in a tactful way."

Angela tells Betty: "When we were able to resolve that conflict, I knew we could handle anything."

They have worked through numerous other conflicts since then. Angela and Betty realize that they actually function better as a team because they acknowledge their differences and deal with them openly, with mutual respect.

6

Here's how Betty puts it: "We've learned a lot from each other because we're not afraid to say, 'Wait a minute! I look at that a different way. Can we talk?'"

Chapter Summary

Even when you're doing everything right in a conflict situation, things may not go exactly as you planned. After all, the other person doesn't have a script to read in response to what you say. So it's best to expect the unexpected.

You can go even further. You can be ready for the unexpected by predicting typical problems and deciding in advance what you'll do. In this chapter, you saw four common pitfalls in conflict resolution. Here, in a nutshell, is how you can cope with these possibilities:

◆ Pitfall 1: Getting Carried Away with Emotions

- Return to the Your Turn step.

- Take more time to listen and defuse the situation.

- Avoid criticizing the person who is extremely emotional.

- Express your own feelings in a responsible way.

- Avoid apologizing for your feelings.

◆ Pitfall 2: Aiming for a Quick "Right" Answer

- Let both sides explain their views completely.

- Identify the validity in the other person's view.

- Combine the two views whenever possible.

- Use brainstorming to develop cooperation.

- Aim for a resolution that both sides "own."

◆ Pitfall 3: Getting Stuck on Positions

- Remember that arguing on positions leads to win/lose.

- Find the common ground.

- Be patient, letting trust and cooperation build.

- Try a time-out to get a fresh perspective.

- Have a third party step in (as a last resort).

◆ Pitfall 4: Breaking Promises

- Always get a clear, specific agreement.

- If the agreement isn't honored, ask directly: "What happened?"

- Express your expectations firmly.

- Play a broken record if necessary.

- State consequences if necessary.

All of these ways to cope with the pitfalls revolve around one main point: implement the Four-Step Process. Continue using the sequence of Your Turn, My Turn, Mutual Planning, and Follow Through. People may not cooperate as quickly as you would like, and they may come up with unexpected comments. But now you have a model for conflict resolution that will take you through even the most difficult conflict situation.

Take a Moment

Is there a conflict in your life right now that you need to resolve? Plan for it below.

Issue: _____

Key person: _____

What you are going to do: _____

_____

A Final Word

Two old gentlemen were talking. One pointed to a shovel and asked, "Does it work?" The other man answered, "If you make it work." Then the first man pointed to a broom and asked, "Does it work?" He received the same answer, "If you make it work." Will any of these skills for managing conflict work? *If you make it work!*

6

Self-Check: Chapter Six Review

Answers to the following questions appear on page 103.

1. True or False?
   Even when you do everything right in conflict resolution, you may still experience pitfalls.

2. True or False?
   When you are emotional during conflict, it's best to apologize for having those feelings.

3. True or False?
   Taking a time out is a good idea when two people are stuck on positions.

4. True or False?
   Call in a third party to resolve a conflict only as a last resort.

5. True or False?
   Describing the consequences of not following through is the same as a threat.

6. True or False?
   You will probably have more conflict in your life in the future—and you will know how to handle it.

Your Action Plan for Managing Workplace Conflict

In future conflicts, which of the items below do you intend to use? Place a check in the box at the left. Indicate if an item is a new skill for you by placing a check in the box at the right.

Use in Future?   **New Skill?**

❑ Analyze the conflict to identify the   ❑
    issue and emotions.

❑ Analyze the conflict to identify   ❑
    the level(s) involved.

❑ Use the "What If?" Game to build courage.   ❑

❑ Speak to the key person.   ❑

❑ Address the conflict within 24 hours.   ❑

❑ Select a neutral place, if possible.   ❑

❑ Use the Four-Step Process:
    Your Turn   ❑
    My Turn   ❑
    Mutual Planning   ❑
    Follow Through   ❑

❑ Use special skills when necessary:
    Sorting   ❑
    Fogging   ❑
    Time Out   ❑
    Broken Record   ❑
    Request   ❑
    Flushing   ❑

6

Answers to Selected Exercises

Chapter One

Chapter Review (page 19)

1. a. It's not "nice" to have conflict.
    b. Conflict is the same as a fight (win/lose result).
    c. A true team experiences only harmony, never conflict.

2. Any four of these are correct answers:
    Firecracker
    Cold shoulder
    Backstabbing
    Memory lane
    Social zinger
    Trivia fights
    Having the last word

3. All of these are potential benefits of conflict.

4. Issues
    Future
    Solutions

Chapter Two

Types of Conflict: Your Turn to Analyze (page 32)

Conflict 1 is Type 1: Conflict over facts or data.
Ideas for Action: Donald and Ernie need to talk about their different versions of when the inspection is scheduled. They need to determine which version is most reliable.
Additional Possibilities: This conflict also has some aspects of Type 3: Conflict over process or methods. The argument touches on *how* Donald should spend his time.

Conflict 2 is Type 2: Conflict over process or methods.
Ideas for Action: Since the issue is how to proceed with the landscape project, the customer needs to hear the ways in which exterior planting differs from interior. But it will also be worth considering why the customer prefers to stick with the person he or she has worked with before.

Conflict 3 is Type 4: Conflict over values.

Ideas for Action: Recognize how deeply Betsy believes in this cause. Give her time to explain her belief. Even if you need to make restrictions based on company rules, show respect for her views.

Additional Possibilities: Type 1 facts or data may be involved here, too, as Betsy may not understand the company rules about collecting donations.

Chapter Review (page 35)

1. Perceive their goals as incompatible.

2. The issue
   The emotions

3. Type 1: Conflict over facts or data
   Type 2: Conflict over process or methods
   Type 3: Conflict over purpose
   Type 4: Conflict over values

4. Type 2: Conflict over process or methods

Chapter Three

Take a Moment (page 39)

1. I'd like to hear your side of the story.

2. Help me understand where you got your information.

3. Can you help me find any holes in my logic?

Chapter Review (page 50)

1. Responsibility
   Relationship
   Real Problem

2. It unites everyone on the team.
   OR
   It gets us all on the same side.

3. Who?
   When?
   Where?

4. Key

5. 24

Chapter Four

Chapter Review (page 70)

1. Your Turn
   My Turn
   Mutual Planning
   Follow Through

2. It gets both people on the same side (cooperating).
   OR
   It generates many possibilities OR keeps us from seeking a "right" answer too soon.

3. Positions
   Common ground

4. Synergy, creativity, high-level communication skills

Chapter Five

Take a Moment (page 76)

1. I'll ask Brian to return your call.

2. The new software isn't here yet. It should be here tomorrow.

3. The figures are correct. I checked with accounting.

Take a Moment (page 83)

1. Fogging

2. Sorting

3. Flushing

Chapter Review (page 86)

1. a. Ignore part of the communication.

2. a. Vague acknowledgement.

3. a. The time to resume.

4. a. Persistence.

5. c. "I want . . ."

6. b. Truth.

Chapter Six

Chapter Review (page 98)

1. True

2. False

3. True

4. True

5. False

6. True